PRAISE FOR *TA ECONOMICS*

C000070261

"In a perpetual global war for talent, it is easy to get lost in the daily skirmishes. In *Talent Economics*, Gyan Nagpal accomplishes two rare things... provides a global battle plan and the specific tactics that can translate into success in today's high growth markets. Truly, this book is an important addition to the talent conversation." **Rebecca Ray, Senior Vice President and Head – Global Human Capital, The Conference Board**

"This book is astonishing in its breadth and scope. It is a thoroughly entertaining read, filled with real-life case studies and nuggets of historical fact." **Govind Karunakaran, Chief Executive Officer, grupokaybee**

"Finally a business book I read cover to cover. *Talent Economics* is a good blend of intriguing and relevant data, with practical approaches to creating talent strategies that are relevant to both large globally dispersed corporations and smaller locally contained companies. As I was reading I was immediately thinking of ways to apply some of the strategies to my current challenges at making talent management more real and impactful in my current organization. Simple concepts for an increasingly complex world – my kind of book." **Timothy Huiting, Director, People and Organization Capability, Microsoft India**

"For those serious about developing a talent strategy, the book should serve as a valuable reference and guide." **Yeo Keng Choo, Managing Director, Caliper Singapore**

"This book will be particularly valued by those working in multi-cultural and multi-national enterprises. It looks at both broad concepts and ideas and gets into the detail of tackling the issues." **Christopher Bennett , Director, BPA Australasia and Board Member, Center for Non-Profit Leadership**

Talent
Economics

For Sherry – my inspiration,
and Nandini – my anchor.

Talent
Economics
The fine line between winning and losing the global war for talent

Gyan Nagpal

KoganPage

LONDON PHILADELPHIA NEW DELHI

First published in Great Britain and the United States in 2013 by Kogan Page Limited

120 Pentonville Road
London N1 9JN
United Kingdom
www.koganpage.com

1518 Walnut Street, Suite 1100
Philadelphia PA 19102
USA

4737/23 Ansari Road
Daryaganj
New Delhi 110002
India

© Gyan Nagpal, 2013

The right of Gyan Nagpal to be identified as the author of this work has been asserted by him in accordance with the Copyright, Designs and Patents Act 1988.

ISBN   978 0 7494 6848 4
E-ISBN   978 0 7494 6849 1

British Library Cataloguing-in-Publication Data

A CIP record for this book is available from the British Library.

Library of Congress Cataloging-in-Publication Data

Nagpal, Gyan.
   Talent economics : the fine line between winning and losing the global war for talent / Gyan Nagpal.
      p. cm.
   Includes bibliographical references and index.
   ISBN 978-0-7494-6848-4 – ISBN 978-0-7494-6849-1   1. Manpower planning.   2. Personnel management.   3. Intellectual capital–Management.   4. Human capital–Management.   I. Title.
   HF5549.5.M3N155 2012
   658.3–dc23
                                                                                    2012032016

Typeset by Graphicraft Limited, Hong Kong
Printed and bound in Great Britain by Ashford Colour Press Ltd

For more information visit: **www.TalentEconomics.com**:

to subscribe to the monthly Talent Economics newsletter;

to take a free edition of the PeopleLENS survey, and benchmark your organization's talent strategy;

to track emerging research on talent economics and people strategy.

CONTENTS

ACKNOWLEDGEMENTS

It took three eventful years to research, write and rewrite this book, and there are a great many that carried me along the way. So before we begin, I'd like to thank: CJ Hwu, for gifting me the first few insights on the journey an idea must take to reach your hands today; the Jacaranda Books team: Jayapriya Vasudevan, for being no less than my guardian angel and Priya Doraswamy, for your commercial savvy; Noel Hadden, for your friendship and support in the crucial early months that helped me take on this mountain; Rajashree Srinivasan, for being an able research associate, and making such good sense of PeopleLENS data from over 180 companies; four exemplary global leaders I constantly thought of when writing this book: Sanjiv Malhotra, Noni Lowenstein, Tim Huiting and Martin Moehrle – having watched you work at very close quarters, I know how each of you personifies the very ethos of 21st-century leadership; Matthew Smith and the entire team at Kogan Page Publishing – for being the most entrepreneurial, flexible and efficient partners an author could wish for.

ABOUT THE AUTHOR

Gyan Nagpal is an award winning talent strategist and leadership coach, who is deeply invested in researching changes to the global talent pool. Currently based in Singapore, over the last decade he has helped some of the world's largest organizations build significant business franchises across the Asia Pacific Region. As CEO and Principal at PeopleLENS Global Associates, Gyan trains and coaches leaders on their role as talent champions; and travels the world speaking on leadership and talent topics. You can follow his work at **www.PLGAonline.com**.

Introduction

Every book like every tree, germinates from a seed. Some grow from an idea, others because a great story needs to be told. This one came from a question. Why are we still at war?

Close to 15 years after Steve Hankin at McKinsey & Company first coined the term 'war for talent', we see no end to this competition for capability. Executives have long woken up to the fact more than anything else, it is the quality of a workforce that makes a company great. Yet in spite of frantic efforts to woo the best and brightest, and pamper the high potential, most companies find themselves haemorrhaging talent to competition in good years and then choosing to lay off precious talent in bad ones. A lose–lose proposition if I ever saw one.

The reality is that business cycles are getting more volatile, and organizations coming to terms with a globally connected world are faced with unprecedented risks. Researching and writing this book was an attempt to bring these two management issues together. My goal was to understand how economic volatility and talent management could form part of the same equation. There is economic value in this insight, and my conversations showed that we clearly need it.

One leader I asked offered a vehement opinion: 'Our only answer is to recognize the economic value of talent today – we have to pay them more.' 'Well, the investment banks tried that, and it made matters worse,' was my response. One head of HR I spoke to said: 'We are responding by strengthening our talent management processes and software.' It was clear that a fresh perspective was needed. You see, we continue to look at the competition for talent as a problem that needs a solution. Take the example of a gorilla that has grown too big for its cage – we are looking to fix the gorilla, and not the cage.

The fine line, therefore, between winning and losing the global war for talent is a mental one. We each need to cross this fine line. It is what separates the problematic abnormal from the 'new normal'.

In the future, the data tells us, this war for talent will get considerably worse, because while the global circumstances for business are converging, the 3-billion-strong global workforce is not. In some places it is ageing rapidly, in others, social, cultural or language barriers are holding talent back. And in countries full of young personal ambition, a lack of infrastructure or education is severely limiting potential.

In today's global marketplace, decision makers are increasingly recognizing the need for a proactive talent strategy, one that balances short-term 'binge and purge' tendencies with long-term pipeline development. Or for that matter, they are recognizing the need for talent strategy that balances global ambition with the vastly divergent ground realities in Seattle, Seville or Shanghai. And that is just the macro reality.

At a micro level too, there is change. The employee is evolving, and hence the very concept of employment must evolve to keep pace. If not, managers who use supervisory mindsets and mechanisms framed in the middle of the 20th century seriously risk disconnecting their own professional lifeline. On the following pages, we examine all these trends, macro and micro.

I strongly believe in enquiry before advocacy, and this book follows the same principle. So we will spend the first half capturing key global trends, before examining the numbers; and then invest the second half exploring, forecasting and strategizing. As a reader of business books, I most enjoy those written in a plain hand, an informal tone and simple English – the kind that could be read on aeroplanes or beaches, as well as in offices. So I have tried to give you the same, leaving most of the jargon out – except in areas where it's unavoidable, and for this I ask your forgiveness.

I do hope that *Talent Economics* will make you think. And act.

Complexity, economics and 21st-century globalization

> 'It doesn't matter how much you want. What really matters is how much you want it. The extent and complexity of the problem does not matter as much as does the willingness to solve it.' **RALPH MARSTON**

The world as we know it today

As any perfectionist will tell you, grocery shopping can be an exceptionally stressful experience these days. On a recent visit to an East London supermarket, looking at ingredients for a quick supper, I added up no less than 68 different kinds of pasta sauce on one aisle, and not 10 steps away, a bewildering assortment of pasta to choose from. Somewhere north of 170 options were neatly organized along a 40-foot shelf – ribbon, noodle, short, tubular, minute, stuffed, sheet; all available in durum, organic, wholewheat, buckwheat, gluten free, low GI... you get the picture. Apart from the fact that I had 11,560 or more pasta combinations to decide from for my humble meal that night, the experience itself was sweetly symbolic of life today. The world we live in today is an increasingly complex one.

Complexity isn't a new phenomenon, and certainly not new to management practice – but it is getting more and more difficult to answer even some basic questions, such as: What does the leader of tomorrow look like? What is the new definition of long term (given we will see more systemic change over the next 10 years than we saw in the last 20)? Is the concept of retirement still relevant?

In a world more connected and wired than ever before, we have more information and fewer answers. This is because a pond full of information can sometimes be less useful than a cup full of insight.

This book is all about insight. It is about how the great global organizations of tomorrow can develop the leaders, the managers or the workers they need to fuel growth. It's also about how we can counter global complexity, to improve the way our organizations work and succeed. And finally, when what we know changes faster and faster, it is about building an organization that thrives on learning and enquiry.

It does so using two totally unrelated disciplines. The first is the fundamental economics of talent management, both the macro realities of demand against supply and the micro truth of how the basic employer–employee contract is changing. The second is rediscovering talent strategy – not the laundry list of HR initiatives for the year but true, commercial strategy that sits right at the top of the boardroom agenda.

Before pulling out into traffic, a quick glance over the shoulder is always a good idea. So before we script strategy for what we often call our most important resource, it would be prudent to acknowledge the mega trends that got us to where we are today – smack in the middle of a global war for talent.

Globalization – through the rear-view mirror

The earliest documented evidence of a commercially connected world is found in travellers' tales describing mercantile trade routes to China. A few centuries before Christ, merchants seeking silk, spice, tea and rare pottery built a flourishing trade back in Europe. And global business began.

Many centuries later, 'around the world' sea routes helped create a whole new breed of superpowers with colonial ambitions. Trade flourished, as did the economies of countless ports, principalities and nations en route. Business and adventure had been inextricably linked and, over the next 400 years, the art of scouring the world for differentiated products (or better value) to meet consumption demand proved incredibly lucrative business.

And that brings us to the 20th century, where humankind rewrote the laws of interaction and commerce. From commercial telephony to broadcasting or air travel to the internet; innovation and commerce changed consumption patterns, improved our general awareness of the planet and reshaped the way we correlate as a species. This all happened before 1990.

For the purpose of this book, I want to focus on what people involuntarily achieved over the last 3,704 days of the last century – roughly the last 10 years and a sneeze. During this period, if it were possible, the economic world changed course 'on a dime' and scripted its most definitive decade. If we attempt to draw a thread between economics and literature, it would be analogous to an author rewriting the whole plot in the last chapter of the book. And, though no one could have predicted it then, the first domino tipped on 9 November 1989.

The wall that rewrote economics

On that day in 1989, the fall of the Berlin wall created a 'unipolar' world for the first time in recent economic history. Few had seen it coming, but economic growth without institutional strength had made the Soviet dream too large and unmanageable for much of the 1980s. Finally, it took a mix of a stalled economy, a dramatic slump in oil prices and a severe grain shortage to unscrew the last hinge that kept the USSR together. As Russia braced for large-scale famine; a wall and an ideology were together a small trade-off for the US $100 billion lifeline the Soviet bloc desperately needed to avoid imminent social catastrophe.

And with that – the proverbial dime – capitalism became the default global economic philosophy. Claiming ideological victory, it hasn't taken long since then for governments and companies, in both free markets and controlled economies alike, to flatten the world for profit.

The significance of events in 1989 is huge, as the loss of the Berlin wall also meant the prospective integration of Russia and Eastern Europe into the global marketplace. Yet, in only the 20-odd years since the wall came down we have seen a number of other significant developments with worldwide consequences for business.

I'd like to focus on three in this book. I call them 'the T^3 multiplier':

$$\text{Tiger economies} \times \text{Technology ubiquitousness} \times \text{Talent commoditization}$$

Why do I call them the T^3 multiplier, you may ask? Because when captured in the same frame, they collectively paint the picture going forward – the picture of 21st-century globalization.

Tiger economies and the new global landscape

Since the demise of the USSR, nothing has challenged the 'market share' of the free market system quite like China and India. Both countries offer us a study in contrast, yet at the deepest level share two dramatic similarities: one, their social fabric comes woven of the same socialist loom, and two, they possess some of the most ambitious young talent in the world today. And they do not have this in small measure. For every three workers in the rest of the world, there is an Indian and a Chinese.

As emerging economic titans, it might serve us well to reacquaint with what has happened in both India and China over the past 20 years. Given their 3,000-year-old history, this might seem like a veritable blink of an eye.

Consuming itself out of poverty – the Indian rebirth

In 1991, India weathered a precipitous balance of payments crisis, which reduced its proud but closed 'mixed' economy (part private, part government owned) to its knees. Brought on by a number of internal and external geopolitical factors, which had caused spiralling debt, India's sovereign creditworthiness that year was downgraded to non-investment grade. International investment capital started to fly out the door and the only way to stop the haemorrhage was an expensive bridge loan from the IMF and World Bank.

This loan came at a price, with the real cost being a commitment by India's government to drop trade restrictions, lower import tariffs, open up the economy and integrate its market with the rest of the world. An increasingly integrating global economy suddenly had 800 million new consumers.

What we have since seen unfold in India over the last 20 years has been game changing for business. Here was an inefficient democracy, riddled with corruption, poverty and illiteracy, but with one of the most 'aspirational' populations in the world. Such is the power of entrepreneurial energy and aspiration in India that the bulk of its economic growth doesn't come from capital investments (as in most other emerging markets), but is driven primarily by private enterprise and private consumption.

Three inferences from research carried out for McKinsey & Company and published in 2007, capture the country's unique march out of poverty, and its future potential quite accurately:

'India's rapid economic growth has set the stage for fundamental change among the country's consumers. The same energy that has lifted hundreds of millions of Indians out of desperate poverty is creating a massive middle class centred in the cities...

... If India continues its recent growth, average household incomes will triple over the next two decades and it will become the world's 5th-largest consumer economy by 2025, up from 12th now...

... India will witness the rapid growth of its middle class – households with disposable incomes from 200,000 to 1,000,000 rupees a year. That class now comprises about 50 million people, roughly 5 per cent of the population. By 2025 a continuing rise in personal incomes will spur a tenfold increase, enlarging the middle class to about 583 million people, or 41 per cent of the population' (Beinhocker, Farrell and Zainulbhai, 2007).

In many strategy circles, India represents the greatest long-term opportunity for business since 1900, when a similar set of aspirations and consumption conditions helped shape the destiny of another global giant – the United States.

Age-old Chinese wisdom

A study in contrast to India, China's story has been equally arresting. In the early 1980s, soon after Chairman Mao's death, China started untying its bamboo curtain. The next 10 years saw a quiet tiptoe transformation from authoritarian Maoist doctrine to the 'socialist market economy' that it is today. But it wasn't until the new constitution of the Communist Party of China was published in late 1992, under Deng Xiaoping's leadership, that the true manifesto for change was outlined to the world. China was looking to upgrade, with controlled intent, and on a scale seldom seen. Modernization was sought in four areas:

- agriculture;
- science and technology;
- industry;
- the military.

Deng's strategy was as simple as it was elegant. One of the first steps – setting up the first Special Economic Zones in Guangdong and Fujian provinces during the early 1980s – set up a controlled environment for the business world to engage China. It was, in many ways, like hosting a party on the front porch; a welcoming gesture and demonstrating a willingness to socialize, yet keeping the house (and the treasures it held) securely locked away.

China's approach to agricultural reforms around the same time was also in stark contrast to the Soviet belief in state-owned farming. In 1979 China agreed to lease out parcels of land to households for farming. The results were immediate. Between 1979 and 1983 agricultural output rose by 7 per cent per year. Soviet farming output, on the other hand, continued its struggle with low output and bureaucracy, a move which eventually led to the great grain shortage mentioned earlier.

China's progressive and deliberate path in the 1990s led to the setting up of the country's first stock exchange in Shenzhen, a gradual disinvestment in state-owned enterprise, accelerated foreign investment into the country and reduction of trade barriers. By the time China crossed a major milestone by joining the WTO in 2001, China's economic miracle was here to stay.

In more recent times China is talking about labour reforms – including a statutory minimum wage and regulating work hours for wage earners. Further, before it truly opens its house of treasures, it is investing heavily in higher education and foreign language capability within the Chinese workforce.

The tiger economies, India and China, are important dimensions of the world business order, but have only just started playing out for the vast majority of organizations that claim to be global. They both pose a unique set of challenges to the way business leaders would ideally like their operations run. For a start, foreign exchange and licensing controls still exist in both economies, as does a formidable bureaucracy. In addition, the chaos brought on by rapid and uneven growth can be very distracting, as is amply demonstrated in the case of Jim Holden, described below.

CASE STUDY

On a 2000 visit to India, Jim Holden, the CEO of Chrysler, looked at the poor state of roads and decided that his company would not pursue India as a potential market. India built 517,957 cars that year, less than a tenth of the number produced in the United States – then the world's largest car market (see **http://oica.net/category/production-statistics/2000-statistics/**).

Only nine years later (in 2009), India built 2,166,238 road cars, up 17.3 per cent on 2008 numbers. In what was a very tough year for the US auto industry (and which required severe inventory reduction), the corresponding number in the United States was 2,246,410 – down 40.5 per cent year on year. Incidentally, in April 2009, President Obama announced that Chrysler was filing for Chapter 11 bankruptcy protections.

Together India and China have rebalanced the world. Recent GDP forecasts reveal that the 2008–09 financial crisis has shaved a full 10 years off initial estimates of when the global economy will be split equally between the developed and the developing. A few years ago, the accepted date was somewhere towards 2020 – but the 2009–10 slowdown in many Western markets has ensured that half the world's GDP today comes from the developed world and the other half from the developing one. And this isn't a static picture. In 2000 this ratio stood at 60:40 in favour of developed economies. By 2020, estimates point to an inverse ratio.

The world in 2020

'So give me a turbulent world as opposed to a quiet world and I'll take the turbulent one.' ANDY GROVE

To help paint a picture of how the next phase of globalization will reshape our talent landscape, let's start by first revisiting the definition of what we call a 'global organization'. This is fundamental to getting the most out of this book because, as current strategy (or lack of strategy) reveals, many companies that call themselves global have yet to come to grip with what 'business 2020' and beyond will look like.

Early into the 2020 decade, China will become the world's largest economy in purchasing power parity (PPP) ie price neutral terms, and by 2035 or so, India will overtake the United States to claim position number 2. Along the way, we will have the odd date adjustment, bubble and crisis or two, but the fact that this will happen is inevitable. The inherent consumption economics, personal aspiration and committed investments in both economies are too strong for it not to. The Euromonitor International chart shown in Table 1.1 lists the top 10 economies as they stood at the end of 2010 and the predictions for 2020.

Multiple sources of economic research suggests the United States will still lead the world on wealth creation among the large economies, and Japan will continue at its current low growth trajectory, but the growth of consumption in countries such as India and China (on the scale at which these two economies operate) promise to be nothing short of breathtaking.

No longer an option

Large global companies chasing double-digit returns to shareholders and the number 1, 2 or 3 positions in their industry will have no option but to be present and participate economically in the world's large principal economies. How can they avoid it and still stay globally competitive? In 2020, in a world more connected than ever, the top four nations will represent 55 cents for every dollar of

TABLE 1.1 The 10 largest economies by GDP in PPP terms: 2010 and 2020 (US $ millions)

Ranking	2010		2020	
	Country	GDP (I$ million)	Country	GDP (I$ million)
1.	USA	14,802,081	China	28,124,970
2.	China	9,711,244	USA	22,644,910
3.	Japan	4,267,492	India	10,225,943
4.	India	3,912,991	Japan	6,196,979
5.	Germany	2,861,117	Russia	4,326,987
6.	Russia	2,211,755	Germany	3,981,033
7.	United Kingdom	2,183,277	Brazil	3,868,813
8.	France	2,154,399	United Kingdom	3,360,442
9.	Brazil	2,138,888	France	3,214,921
10.	Italy	1,767,120	Mexico	2,838,722

SOURCE: Euromonitor International from IMF, International Financial Statistics and World Economic Outlook / UN / national statistics.

economic activity on the planet. We haven't even begun adding Brazil, Russia, Thailand, Malaysia, Turkey or Peru to this list, all of which are predicted to grow faster than the world average, or the other 30-odd emerging economies including populous markets such as Vietnam, Mexico, Argentina, Egypt, Indonesia or South Africa for that matter.

There is another dimension beyond geography that companies must consider carefully, as the aggregate GDP numbers barely tell half the story. What will this increased production really mean to the average Joe (or for that matter Maki, Ramesh or Wei-Ling) in

TABLE 1.2   Forecast per capita GDP in 2020 and projected economic growth 2010–20 for the top four economies

Country	2020 per capita GDP (I$ – PPP terms)	Projected growth 2010–20
China	18,637	147%
USA	69,888	48%
India	7,221	119%
Japan	47,297	40%

SOURCES: UN Population projections, IMF and World Bank research.

lifestyle and consumption terms? The answer could lie in looking at GDP numbers in terms of economic activity per head – in other words, per capita production. As we did above, we need to cancel out the relative bias created by different currencies, to achieve PPP. This creates a level playing field to analyse consumption patterns and lifestyle dynamics.

Looking at the four largest global economic theatres over the next decade – China, the United States, India and Japan – Table 1.2 shows the forecasted per capita numbers for 2020.

On the one hand Table 1.2 tells us that economic activity in the world's two largest emerging economies is set to double, on the other hand we see a whole new consumption distribution emerge between the four heavy hitters. In other words, by 2020, the new world consumption axis (across the top four economies) could look something like Figure 1.1.

18 – 69 – 7 – 47. These numbers live at the core of 21st-century globalization. They reflect a brand new 'multipolarity' set to emerge by 2020. Unlike the last time – during the Cold War – when differences in political and economic ideology played out at a macro level, this time global organizations need to anticipate a distinct micro-divergence. This is a divergence in lifestyle economics, where the same set of needs are expressed at three or maybe even four different price points.

FIGURE 1.1   Forecast per capita GDP at PPP for the top four
economies in 2020 (all figures in thousand I$)

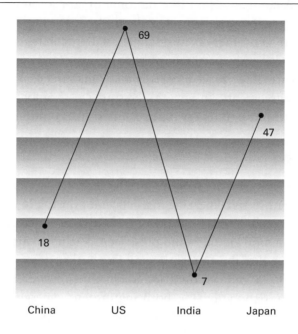

In a globally connected world driven equally by the rich and the
rising, we see four or more fundamentally different consumption
patterns driving global economic behaviour. The implications for
business are huge. And the issue threatens to change the fundamental
definition of a global organization. If multinational companies today
want to be global companies tomorrow, they will need different
approaches to product development, different approaches to innovation and different management approaches to what we see commonly
today. So by definition, a 'truly global' firm in 2020 should have the
ability to be domestically relevant to consumers in both developed
and developing markets – at the same time.

The state of current strategy

If we analyse the current set of companies operating across both
developed and emerging markets, we see three 'broad bucket' business strategies in popular use.

Strategy A

A strategy A company is an international organization motivated to exist in emerging economies principally through a **cost play**. This could be through low-cost manufacturing, material procurement or sourcing of services. Common artefacts of such a business include offshore factories, back-office service centres and outsourced manufacturing or services agreements. In general, a strategy A company still earns 75 per cent or more of its revenue from a primary 'home' market.

Strategy B

Strategy B organizations are motivated to generate significant revenue from both mature and emerging markets, but principally via a **product play**. Tactics include distribution of a similar product globally and creating a common global brand presence. To achieve this, a company may invest in distribution and retail networks, possess significant staff strength in many countries and sometimes even base core functions internationally – in both mature and emerging countries. For a company like this, 40–60 per cent of revenues may come from overseas and emerging markets, supplementing an already healthy home-market revenue stream.

Strategy C

Strategy C is followed in organizations that innovate and tailor products in specific response to market realities. This could mean having an entirely different product or brand strategy for each type of market. These firms tend to be deeply embedded in high-growth economies, with differentiated products that compete across a broad price spectrum. Let's call this a **market play**. Tactics here include building local brands, a distribution presence in smaller towns and cities and hiring senior local leaders with significant autonomy to drive product strategy. In this case a majority of revenues (60–70 per cent) may come from non-traditional (ie other than home) markets.

What we also see in practice, is that the A, B and C strategies are progressive and complementary. A company following strategy A, by definition, will not have significant product distribution or dedicated innovation strategies for the emerging economies in which it operates a manufacturing plant or back office. An example could be the retail giant Costco. A major player in mature markets such as the United States and the United Kingdom, Costco sources many of its bulk packaged products from emerging economies, yet doesn't participate in many emerging economies. Further, Costco's retail approach doesn't match the shopping patterns of less-affluent countries where smaller sized products or packaging are more popular.

But in most cases, companies who chose strategy B will invariably also have the virtues of strategy A in play. This will mean that low-cost manufacturing or back-office operations are also part of the company's overall strategy while it goes about creating a retail presence for global products in emerging and mature markets. Hence strategy B includes strategy A. A good example is Dell Computers, which offers its hugely successful range of servers, desktops and laptop computers across the world and in many emerging markets. Dell products' features and price point are broadly consistent irrespective of where they are sold. The bulk of Dell's manufacturing is done in Greater China, and Dell has sprawling technical support centres in India.

In the same vein, most companies that follow strategy C also adopt strategies A and B in their overall approach. This template currently demonstrates the greatest commitment to building a truly global organization. It also represents the best strategic balance between global production synergies and investment or consumption opportunities in both the emerging and developed world. A very good example of strategy C can be seen in the way the global brand giant, Unilever, runs its business.

CASE STUDY

Unilever has headquarters in the Netherlands and is an early mover into emerging markets. Over half of its employees are based in Asia, Africa and other emerging markets. Coefficently, close to 50 per cent of Unilever's revenue comes from Brazil, India, Indonesia, Turkey, South Africa, China, Mexico, Russia and other emerging countries. Unilever's manufacturing is distributed globally and many brands have been created or customized for the market they are sold in. Unilever is locally relevant and has strong local management structures in both India and China, a situation that should serve the company well, given the 2020 scenario we reviewed.

Strategies A, B and C represent a continuum on which most multi-nationals reside. Since many of these institutions have been built on generations of good strategic choices, it would stand to reason they would want to exploit opportunities inherent in the 2020 global economy. Yet the biggest enemy here is what I call the inertia of success, which comes primarily from an attachment to current structures, management styles, products and technology.

CASE STUDY

Anil K Gupta, the Chair in Global Strategy & Entrepreneurship at the Smith School of Business, The University of Maryland, and a guru on global business strategy has observed this divergence of approach in practice. In a path-breaking book, Gupta and his co-author Haiyan Wang observe:

> 'By our estimates, less than one tenth of the world's five hundred largest companies have even a close to a robust strategy for either China or India, let alone both. By robust strategy, we mean a strategy that is fundamentally market driven (What do the customers in China and India need?) rather than product driven (How can we sell our current products and services in China and India?)' (Gupta and Wang, 2009).

Based on Gupta and Wang's comments and my own research, over the last decade of the 20th century a quantitative distribution of globalized organizations could be represented as shown in Figure 1.2.

The world on the horizon though, looks very different. With more than half the world's GDP at stake, ambitious global companies competing for shareholders' attention will have no option but to adopt strategy C approaches. The future graph could look something like Figure 1.3.

This change will undoubtedly reshape the current DNA of a successful global business entity. Management styles will need to change, as will current approaches to manage resources, including the most critical one – talent.

FIGURE 1.2   Market strategy footprint 2000–10

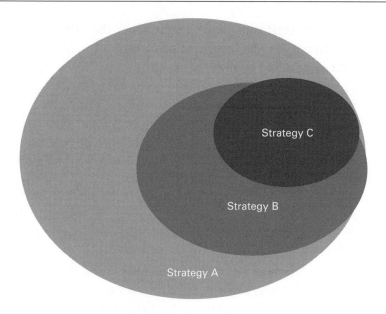

FIGURE 1.3   Market strategy footprint 2020 and beyond

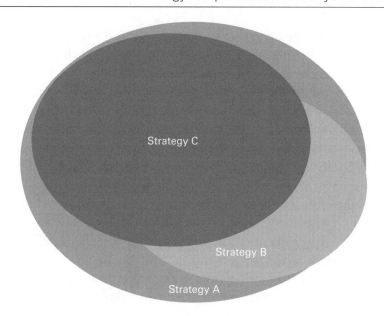

Technology ubiquitousness in a wired world

Most revolutions start small and simmer under the surface gathering strength, adding to an ideology, gaining favourable opinion, first as a credible alternative and then as the majority view. The humble steam engine triggered the first industrial revolution. Information technology prompted the next and there are no history books to prove it – yet.

No force is altering the boundaries of business faster than electronic commerce and the evidence is probably in your hands right now. If you bought a paper copy of this book, it's likely you are already in the minority.

In terms of history, this has all happened in a blink of an eye. Portable connectivity or mobile computing, which boomed with the availability of commercially affordable laptops a couple of decades ago, quickly accelerated innovation in the areas of information portability and eventually mobile convergence. Subsequent inflection points included the opening up of the internet to the public in 1992 and commercial firewall technology that helped companies keep both data and communications private.

Virtual custom

From the customer's perspective, until recently, it's been more smoke and less fire. The internet economy has promised much over the last 20 years, but the 2000 dot com bust sent the industry back to the drawing board, for newer and better commercial architecture.

Virtual custom in itself isn't exactly new. It has been around successfully for over 60 years, with mail orders and telesales being the two predominant channels. Recent numbers, though, indicate we are finally on the cusp of change – both mail order sales and telesales have begun to lose ground rapidly. Innovations in secure payment technology and the increasing development of web 2.0 platforms have finally made online sales wildly profitable. In the near future, I wonder if online multi-dimensional sales experiences, currently being tested on SecondLife and similar wired social platforms, could do the unthinkable – challenge and replace the holy grail of retail: face-to-face selling. For more commoditized products, I cannot see why not.

Virtual work

From the workforce's perspective, virtual work and remote computing has begun to make an impression on the way we work – albeit slowly – because of archaic supervisory mindsets that have refused to relent. But the cost–benefit equation is getting increasingly difficult to ignore. With cheaper, secure multimedia access now available, flexible working is a credible alternative like never before; and, as recent research proves, employees want this.

In a 2009 study carried out by the telecommunications giant Orange, over 3,000 working adults across the United Kingdom were polled on the impact digital connectivity had on work preferences. The results show quite dramatically that what was merely 'an alternative' a few short years ago has already morphed into a mainstream choice.

In the survey, huge groups of knowledge workers preferred some form of flexible or virtual work. Many were willing to give up perks such as the company car and even take pay cuts if they could work from where they chose. The results also showed that 'Full-time flexible working is most popular amongst 18–24 year olds (23% would choose to work flexibly at all times)' (Orange, 2009). The report goes on to ask 'Is this a possible tipping point?' I believe it is.

Later in this book we examine the impact that newer generations are having on the workplace in greater depth. The way we hire, retain, develop and tap into our younger talent must change – and it must change fast.

In aggregate, what started relatively small 20 years ago will surely reach a boil sometime in the current decade. The latest trends of hardware convergence and mobile connectivity guarantee this. Connectivity is now seamless both with customers and with employees, and all aspects of business are increasingly becoming 24/7.

Futurologist James Bellini, sees the future clearer than most:

'The rapidly emerging digital age is also the "connected" age, a future in which web-based networks and online virtual communities make possible a continuous, worldwide "conversation". This conversation is the marketplace of the future, where the currency is collaboration and the sharing of ideas and experiences – where marketing, selling and customer relationships are developed and embedded through engagement that harnesses these online possibilities. Businesses that ignore its power, risk marginalization, decline and potential commercial annihilation. Connectivity is the vital resource of the future economy' (Bellini, 2009, Foreword to the Orange 2009 study).

Talent commoditization – a supply shift

On the surface, the fundamental employment equation between the individual and the organization remains the same: a salary for output, benefits for belonging and a career for contribution. But in practice, over the last 40 years many underlying employment assumptions have irreversibly changed.

The concept of retirement is one such casualty, although optimistic employees still seem to cling to both the concept and the term. Retirement is defined as 'the withdrawal from active work', with the underlying assumption being an employee's ability to fund post-retirement life. In reality, this promise is more an exception than the norm for a significant bulk of today's non-governmental workforce.

If we turn around, it's easy to see the road that brought us here. First, let's look at employee pensions.

In the 1980s, with company balance sheets weighed down by uncompetitive levels of pension liabilities, finance executives around the world began flaunting graphs loosely resembling 'roadmaps to doom'. The message was clear – unless something could be done to reduce this crippling future liability, mature businesses wouldn't be able to compete against newer and hence, by definition, financially unencumbered rivals. 'Private enterprise can't afford the same terms offered by government jobs' bawled the headline.

The consensus at the time was to pass the market risk of pension investments onto the employee. Many company boards voted during the 1990s to convert historic 'defined benefit' pension plans (where a tenured employee gets a predetermined retirement benefit, for example 66 per cent of the base salary earned in the final year of employment) into 'defined contribution' arrangements (where the company contributes a predetermined monthly sum into the employee's personal pension account and passes on responsibility for funding retirement to the employee).

INSEAD Professor J Stewart Black has studied this phenomenon and agrees: 'As recently as 1985, over 70 per cent of non-government organizations had defined retirement benefit programs and only

30 per cent had defined contribution programs. Today the number is reversed' (Stewart Black, 2009).

At first this seemed like a win–win result. Employees felt in greater control of their outcome and balance sheets started looking healthier. In consequence though, it contributed materially to the birth of the global 'war for talent' waging from Seattle to Shanghai today.

Over the last 30 years, with greater monetization and portability of benefits, a critical ingredient of an enduring employment agreement – retirement income – was no longer a function of loyalty to one employer. Talent had truly become portable. Consequently, **'experience' when no longer a measure of security, becomes what it is now – freely exchangeable currency.** Employees can now monetize their value, and seek better pay and benefits elsewhere, and this makes perfect sense, as the employee alone is responsible for funding his or her retirement needs and lifestyle.

In 2010, the consequences of this shift were clear for everyone to see. In consulting major Towers Watson's 2010 Global Workforce Study, covering 20,000 employees in 22 markets worldwide, three quarters agreed that they alone (and not their employers), were responsible for their financial future and career. However, only half felt confident about being able to shoulder this responsibility (Towers Watson, 2010).

Mankind, as history tells us over and over again, seeks the least painful solution and, as a result, ends up exchanging one problem for another. In this case portable benefits created the competition for talent we see today.

Let's look more closely at the war for talent. In 1998, reflecting on the dramatic challenge organizations were facing in finding and keeping employees, McKinsey published an iconic research paper 'The war for talent'. The paper, which focused exclusively on the US market, highlighted two distinct challenges for business.

The first was a significant demand–supply imbalance, especially in middle and senior roles, that was escalating the competition for talent. McKinsey predicted this would intensify over the next five years, a fact that proved to be true, not just in the United States but in many 'hot markets' across the world.

The second point was that the best organizations can win this war by building a talent mindset – hiring the best, paying performers significantly more, defining and delivering an 'employee value proposition' and, most importantly, identifying and developing talent aggressively. This can be summarized as knowing who your stars are and then investing in them.

The report 'The war for talent' was a bellwether for the talent management movement that followed. It spawned new HR processes, new programmes, fancy designations and an intense desire to build a culture that would attract and retain the best.

We stand on the threshold of the next war for talent. This one, though, is less about employee retention and HR processes. It is more about reinventing employment. The winners will be those who move decisively and fast to establish a brand new set of employment anchors for their business. The losers will try and retrofit old HR policies and arrangements to a radically new talent-value system.

As James Bellini says, rather controversially: 'By 2020 a successful and forward-looking business will have no HQ, probably no CEO and only a fraction of the fixed assets it has today. The "connected" company of the future will be lean, flexible and reliant on a dispersed, connected workforce; software will give way to "anyware"' (Bellini, 2009, Foreword to the Orange 2009 study).

Which gets us to the world of the CEO today.

Purposeful leaders and innovation

02

'*The best vision is insight.*' **MALCOLM FORBES**

A leadership quandary

Most CEOs grapple with complexity on a daily basis. Indeed many would argue that's what they get paid for. But unpredictable macro-economics of recent times have made this a whole new pressure cooker.

A normal day includes reflecting on global competition, technology obsolesence, market volatility, unpredictable cash flows, increased regulatory scrutiny, environmental issues, and that's just on the journey to work. There are many changes to grapple with and just because we have a strategy doesn't mean we can predict the outcome. **Change on one vector, we can track, analyse and sometimes forecast, but when change happens simultaneously on three vectors, or more, it challenges even the most astute.** Quite like the experience of shopping for pasta described in Chapter 1, the options are simply mind-boggling.

I have observed many CEOs respond to complexity by simply working harder. They stay working later at night, spend weeks on the road, and work the Blackberry on weekends. Their best response to a 24/7 world is trying to work 24/7. But is this helping or hurting them?

Every couple of years IBM's Institute of Business Studies publishes 'The global chief executive officer study'. In many ways, this is the world's most comprehensive enquiry into what's on the mind of business leaders, across the world, at that precise moment in time.

The 2010 study involved face-to-face interviews with 1,541 CEOs and general managers, between September 2009 and January 2010. It was aptly titled 'Capitalizing on complexity'. There are two distinct observations in the 2010 report that corroborate what we have just described.

The first is that 60 per cent of CEOs feel they are faced with a 'high/very high' level of complexity and 79 per cent feel this will increase in the next five years. The second is that over half the CEOs interviewed don't feel prepared to handle it.

The research report elaborates: 'Our interviews reveal that CEOs are now confronted with a "complexity gap" that poses a bigger challenge than any other factor we've measured in eight years of CEO research' (IBM Corporation, 2010).

Sam Palmisano, Chairman of IBM, reflects on management complexity by saying: 'We occupy a world that is connected on multiple dimensions and at a deep level a global system of systems. That means, among other things, that it is subject to systems-level failures, which require systems-level thinking about the effectiveness of its physical and digital infrastructures' (IBM Corporation, 2010).

In the following chapters, we take a magnifying glass or a 'people lens' as I like to call it, to understand and deconstruct this 'global system of systems'. The timing is perfect – global talent strategy has never been needed more than it is today. Yet we aren't looking for more HR programmes and practices. We are looking instead for a synthesis of local and global talent priorities – a simple method to:

- identify the operative employment trends that affect our people;
- diagnose talent needs at a granular level;
- encourage innovative approaches to manage a changing workforce;
- inspire broad based action, among local and global leaders alike.

The search for new inspiration

Even a shallow dive into the psyche of a modern day CEO is enough to establish that mastering complexity is a primary goal (IBM Corporation, 2010: 2, 15). We also acknowledge that shifting macro-economics factors are causing greater organizational upheaval, which in turn impacts the ability to plan and execute long-term strategy. In fact, almost 7 in 10 CEOs today believe business cycles have become shorter and entail greater risk than ever before (IBM Corporation, 2010: 17).

The risks can be personal too and best scrutinized by looking at the length of the average leadership tenures. If we look at the 2,500 largest organizations globally, the CEO turnover in this group hovers around 14 per cent annually (*The Economist*, 2010). This number includes CEO changes due to planned succession, retirements or

FIGURE 2.1   CEO turnover rate, 2,500 biggest global public companies, %

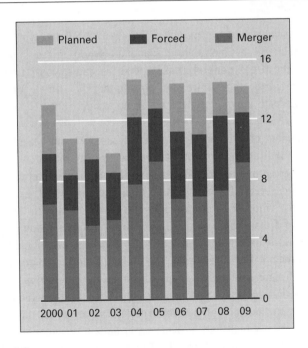

SOURCE: Booz & Company.

fixed-term contracts; as well as forced or involuntary exits due to poor performance, mergers or acquisitions, as shown in Figure 1.2. If, in fact, we agree that much of unplanned turnover has an under-performance bias, the number of leadership dislocations has lived at uncomfortable levels for most of the past decade.

But enhanced risks also present chances for competitive success and opportunities for new thinking and fresh ideas. As we have seen throughout history, ambiguity puts a premium on leadership that can come up with inspired answers.

A Trojan surprise

Most people already know the very popular allegory of the Trojan horse, so below is an abridged summary of its role in the Trojan War.

The Trojan horse

After a nine-year siege on the city of Troy in 1200 BC, the walls of which were considered by many in the ancient world to be impregnable, Odysseus, the Greek general, realized that his battle weary troops were losing heart with the protracted stalemate. The Trojan War, which was littered with incidents of deceit on both sides, showed no signs of ending.

In a moment of cunning stratagem, Odysseus recast his approach to the war, by making the Trojans believe the Greeks had accepted defeat and were withdrawing from battle (they burnt their encampments and pretended to set sail for home). As a final gesture, the Greeks built and gifted a large wooden horse to the Trojans as an offering to the goddess Athena. The Trojan horse, with 30 elite Greek soldiers hidden within its hollow interiors, initially puzzled the Trojan generals, who couldn't decide what to do with it. But, after seeing the burning Greek camp and departing ships, the Trojans dropped their guard. Believing the war was over they unwittingly dragged the horse into the city. That night the hidden Greek soldiers sneaked out under the cover of darkness and opened the city gates. The Greek army, which had furtively crept back after nightfall, was thus able to slip into the city and take the Trojans by surprise – ending the war in a matter of hours.

The situation Odysseus found himself in 3,200 years ago isn't completely dissimilar to what a modern-day CEO faces. As organizational troops today deal with greater volatility and competitive tension, they look to their leaders for breakthrough ideas. Many would argue this is the leader's job. In prospect, every CEO is expected to pull out a few inspired decisions, like metaphorical rabbits from a magician's hat.

21st-century leadership purpose

At the heart of a CEO's decision model and espoused strategy lives leadership purpose. Leadership purpose is an all-encompassing superset of vision, focus, values, learning, conditioning, goal orientation and time reference. A leader needs to have this, as it provides both anchor and compass to weather short-term challenges and navigate towards long-term success.

One way to clarify leadership purpose is to ask the question: What are the one or two business priorities you hold sacrosanct? Are customer satisfaction, shareholder returns, product innovation or employee morale in your top two?

One purposeful leader who has changed how his company operates at its core is Vineet Nayar of HCL.

CASE STUDY   HCL

HCL is an India-based technology company, which was losing market share to bigger rivals when Nayar took over as President in 2005. His route to turn the company around was a unique one. He forged a strategy to change the culture at HCL based on his ideology – that great companies are built around people more than anything else. Nayar calls it 'EFCS' for 'Employee First, Customer Second'. At HCL it is both a philosophy and a galvanizing force, which has not only created more transparency and accountability, but also inverted the pyramid – acknowledging frontline employees as the most important in his organization.

Nayar himself says 'HCL was a traditional pyramid, in which frontline people were accountable to a hierarchy of managers. The hierarchy usually made it more difficult for employees to add value. I began to wonder if we could turn the organization upside down, so that senior management – the heads of enabling functions such as human resources and finance and even the CEO could become accountable to employees' (Nayar, 2010).

It is easy to see Nayar's leadership purpose in every decision he makes and every action he takes. For example, Nayar posted his personal 360° feedback report on the company intranet for every employee to see. Many of his managers followed his lead and did the same. It isn't surprising that HCL doubled its net income within three years of Nayar taking charge.

Indeed, **a leader without purpose is a leader by accident.**

Over the last half century, there have been periods when particular themes of leadership purpose have been popular. During the 1950s through to the 1970s we saw the great leaders of the day obsess about productivity and quality. Almost all management focus centred on improving the firm's footing on both these fronts. Customers gained immensely through process improvements in manufacturing, and the streamlining of services. Japanese total quality management (TQM) was born around this time and thought leaders such as Edwards Deming drove aspirations for process, quality and defect-free manufacturing across the world. During this period, Sony, Toyota and General Motors became role-model organizations, led by purposeful leaders passionate about quality. CEOs such as Akio Morita at Sony helped make 'Made in Japan' synonymous with quality. Similarly, Alfred Sloan's legacy made General Motors the largest global company for years to come.

The winds shifted quite dramatically in the 1980s, and from then until the financial crisis of 2008 we have seen leadership purpose crystallize around shareholder returns. During this period financial markets in general and stock prices in particular drove leadership behaviour like never before, and success for many CEOs was defined in terms of enhanced market value, along with traditional measures such as revenue and profitability. Mergers and acquisition activity also soared, helped along by aggressive investment banking counsel, and so did leverage as a means of growth. In simple terms, leverage denotes the piling on of debt to supplement shareholder capital. It is a common way to expand return on equity, as long as aggregate returns on capital stay above the cost of debt. It wasn't uncommon in the boom years of the late 1990s and mid-2000s to have some organizations (banks being the best example) with leverage ratios of 30 or even 40 (ie US $40 in debt for every US $1 in equity).

The 1990s also marked the time restructuring became wildly popular as a management tool. Hammer and Champy's book *Reengineering the Corporation* provided the framework for proactive organizational renewal. CEOs now had two vectors to deliver greater profitability – increased revenues and market share on one front, and re-engineering efficiencies and cost rationalization on the other.

Citigroup, General Electric and Microsoft were the organizations that defined this era. Sandy Weill of the Traveler's Group and later Citibank, Jack Welch at General Electric and Dick Fuld of Lehman Brothers (ironically Wall Street's longest serving head of a world-class investment bank) were the 'poster CEOs' of this generation, each delivering shareholder value well above market benchmarks.

That was till 2008, when both the financial markets and the value of their companies collapsed. The financial crisis that year also created a crisis of leadership purpose. Many of the aggressive organizations that had delivered above-market returns were exposed as having overextended themselves, thereby risking the fiscal health of a now connected global economy.

Purely chasing shareholder returns is no longer seen as prudent or fashionable because, as we know today, over the last 30 years the very nature of 'the shareholder' has fundamentally changed. The best illustration of this shift comes from the US stock markets. In 1970 individuals owned over 80 per cent of total corporate equity in the United States. Most had personal wealth invested directly in corporate equity, thereby linking their financial destiny directly to the success or failure of a stock. That number had fallen to less than half by 2001, and continues a downward trend (Tonello and Rabimov, 2010). A sizeable bulk of corporate ownership now rests with financial institutions (pension funds, mutual funds, hedge funds, insurance companies, endowments and sovereign wealth funds). If you add on an array of individual speculators who operate in the primary markets today and behave primarily like fair weather investors, most shareholders today have a limited sense of ownership.

As a result, today we see governments, regulators, and management pundits increasingly agree that letting financial markets drive leadership behaviour is analogous to a 'high-carb' diet. It's nothing but an endless cycle of peaks and crashes.

So we stand at the cusp of the next big trend in leadership purpose, and the jury's still out on what future CEOs will draw focus from. However, every early marker points to **innovation** and **collaboration** being front-runners. CEOs everywhere are starting to obsess about disruptive innovation and convergent collaboration as competitive strategies.

CASE STUDY

As part of its 2010 global CEO survey, global consulting major Pricewaterhouse-Coopers (PwC) interviewed Bob McDonald, Procter & Gamble's Chairman, President and CEO. There is one answer from that interview, in particular, I'd like to focus on. When asked specifically about innovation at Procter & Gamble (P&G), Bob's response was: 'Innovation is the lifeblood of our company. We live or die based on the innovation that we do. The good news is that we do have an innovative company. We spend about US $2 billion a year on research and development. That's about 50% more than our closest competitor and more than most of our closest competitors combined' (PwC, 2010).

P&G doesn't just invest 2 billion a year in R&D, but has taken R&D a step further into what internally it calls C&D – 'connect & develop'. This radical programme started by Bob McDonald's predecessor A G Lafley in 2000, aimed to source over half the firm's innovation from outside the company, through tie-ups with other companies or individual innovators. In a 2006 *Harvard Business Review* article, two senior managers of the company's innovation centres, Larry Huston and Nabil Sakkab, spelt out Lafley's transformational challenge and with it the opportunity for P&G:

> 'It was, and still is, a radical idea. As we studied outside sources of innovation, we estimated that for every P&G researcher there were 200 scientists or engineers elsewhere in the world who were just as good – a total of perhaps 1.5 million people whose talents we could potentially use. But tapping into the creative thinking of inventors and others on the outside would require massive operational changes. We needed to move the company's attitude from resistance to innovations "not invented here" to enthusiasm for those "proudly found elsewhere". And we needed to change how we defined, and perceived, our R&D organization – from 7,500 people inside to 7,500 plus 1.5 million outside, with a permeable boundary between them' (Huston and Sakkab, 2006).

Distributed or **open** innovation isn't a radically new concept. In fact it's been around long before Henry Chesbrough, a professor at the University of California, Berkeley, wrote the first book on it in 2003. But it has exploded since then. Most popular with internet enterprises, distributed innovation models thrive in a variety of different industries, from pharmaceuticals to food products to animation. The hi-tech ones commonly call it 'crowd sourcing'. But for the majority of old economy CEOs who grew up thinking innovation must be controlled, this has been a sweet reawakening.

P&G is way ahead of that crowd though, and Bob McDonald reflects on the value this 10-year head start has to P&G's culture of innovation: 'Today, nearly every new item we bring out was produced with at least one partner somewhere in the world. For example, we co-locate scientists from partner organizations and from our organization in the same laboratory. It's amazing what you can do when you knock down the barriers in an organization or the barriers between organizations' (PwC, 2010).

Innovative cultures

Innovation, McDonald believes, should be a matter of life and death for tomorrow's leaders. And with the right sponsors at the top, ideas and innovation can come from anywhere in the organization. A company with 50,000 employees and millions of customer contacts a day can be a hotbed for inventive thinking. Indeed, in a fast-paced world, it would serve this business incredibly well to have 50,000 thinking about how to improve products, processes and customer experiences.

Employee genius

This can only happen through what I call 'cerebral engagement' in the workplace. In other words, this is an organization's ability to engage the ideas hidden within every employee. It goes one step beyond the traditional measures of employee engagement that leaders today focus on – commitment, loyalty or discretionary effort; and several steps beyond old, dusty suggestion boxes. Cerebral engagement is all about innovation and collaboration. It's firstly about employees moving beyond what currently is, and thinking about what could be. It's also about mustering up the courage to offer up ideas for scrutiny or debate (and this isn't easy if the culture doesn't encourage unsolicited ideas in the first place). Finally, it's about giving employees the flexibility and space to follow through an idea with resolute application. In practice, developing and executing a great idea through to monetization often requires working cross-functionally, across organizational boundaries and external margins. Later in this book considerable space is devoted to cerebral engagement and how leaders can use it to fire up innovation across the enterprise. The best ideas are the simple ones and they can come from anywhere. We just need ordinary employees to tap into their genius.

Cerebral engagement is the foundation stone of widespread, self-perpetuating innovation but it cannot deliver outstanding value to customers and shareholders in a vacuum. It can make work fun, but it cannot make a company great. To turn ideas into profit, we need purposeful leaders, who have insight, inspiration and a passion to innovate the enterprise.

Every industry has a thought leader

I'm a big Fastcompany.com fan. A few quick glances at its web pages per week energize me instantly. As I have experienced, just reading through a wealth of great innovation stories and new ideas can be vicariously enjoyable.

CASE STUDY   Fast Company

Fast Company was started in 1995 by Alan Webber and Bill Taylor, both former editors of *Harvard Business Review*, who set out to chronicle how the business world was changing. And what a ride it's been. On the online site alone, every month 4.3 million people log on and spend an average of 6.2 transformational minutes browsing the world of innovation (according to the company's information kit). Of Fast Company's online readers, 7 per cent are owners or CEOs and of its print readers 31 per cent are owners of or partners in their own business.

In most ways Fast Company typifies the innovation ethic that the iconic companies of the future aspire to. It's also one of the best places to go looking for innovation hotspots. Be it in large global organizations or embryonic start-ups crystallizing around a new brainwave, these are places where next-generation leadership purpose is already at play.

Every year Fast Company publishes its list of the 50 most innovative companies. This annual list is peppered with the usual suspects (Apple, Twitter and Facebook occupy the first three spots in the 2011 survey, Google is at number 6, with Microsoft and Amazon.com further down). After all, it's easy to feature on an innovation list if you innovate daily for breakfast – as is the case with these mega successful technology and web enterprises.

The 2011 list also has some surprises, in the shape of more traditional businesses; some in industries that aren't exactly considered cool within the dorm room entrepreneurial set – PepsiCo, Nissan, Burberry or Huawei. Even the Changchun Dacheng Industrial Group and Kosaka Smelting and Refinery made the annual list.

Here's why Fastcompany.com considers these companies pioneering thought leaders. The Fast Company quotes are taken from **www.fastcompany.com/most-innovative-companies/2011/**.

CASE STUDY

Changchun Dacheng Industrial Group

On Changchun Dacheng Industrial Group, Fast Company says:

> 'Tons of agro-waste go up in flames after each corn harvest; China's Changchun Dacheng Industrial Group is working to turn it into lip gloss and liquid detergent. The chemical giant already makes a range of products from cornstarch, including glycols, key ingredients in cosmetics and cleansers that are usually made with petroleum. It has now pioneered a method to turn cornfield debris into glycols. The next challenge: to make the process cost-competitive with the oil-based originals.'

Nissan

> 'Not long ago, Nissan was being pilloried for a lineup with few hybrid options, as well as CEO Carlos Ghosn's stubborn insistence on investing in unproven all-electric technology. Among the skeptics: his own employees. But with the Leaf, Ghosn has proven the naysayers shortsighted, and grabbed the lead for Nissan in the race toward truly sustainable transportation.'

Huawei

> 'Forget 3G and 4G: China's Huawei Technologies leads the market in LTE (long-term evolution), the newest mobile-network standard, and it's working on what it calls '100G' technology to wirelessly transmit massive amounts of data at ultra-high speeds. Such ambition and the commitment of nearly half its staff to R&D have helped Huawei become the world's second-largest telecom-equipment supplier. That most people still haven't heard of it is due largely to its geographic focus; more than 75% of revenue comes from India, China, and Latin America. But it wants to raise its brand recognition – it's introducing an affordable smartphone that it hopes will 'democratize' that technology – and make Huawei a household name.'

PepsiCo

> 'Does better nutrition require curbing our appetites for Cheetos and Fritos and Mountain Dew (oh, my!)? Not if PepsiCo can help it. The snack-food giant recently opened a

clinical research center charged with making its products healthier – slashing fat, sugar, and sodium by as much as 25% in the next 10 years – without changing their taste. Smaller, fast-dissolving salt crystals on chips, for instance, could mean less sodium with the same addictive, salty flavor.'

Burberry

'Scroll the fashions on burberry.com and you'll be hard-pressed to find much evidence of the British luxury label's iconic beige, black and red check. Credit the updated look to CEO Angela Ahrendts, 50, an American who re-energized the 155-year-old company when she took over in 2006. With award-winning Chief Creative Officer Christopher Bailey, 39, she has reinvigorated the once-ubiquitous check and augmented it with edgier styles that have generated annual sales of $2 billion, making Burberry among the world's top five luxury brands.

Not content simply to jettison its stodgy image on the racks, Burberry has also been digitally savvy. In early 2010, Burberry was the first to simulcast its runway shows in 3-D and invited *Elle*'s Joe Zee and blogger Bryanboy to take over its Twitter account to tweet the luxe Prorsum collection. In September, Burberry live-streamed its catwalk show and allowed customers to instantly order runway items via iPads it had set up in stores.

This year, the company is extending its web reach. Noting that Chinese shoppers already account for 30% of sales in its London stores, the brand is targeting them directly by launching a site in China.'

Kosaka Smelting and Refining

'The closest thing we have to modern-day alchemy may be the work of Kosaka Smelting and Refining, the Japanese firm that harvests gold and other valuable metals from old electronics. From used mobile telephones, Kosaka, a unit of the metals-and-mining company Dowa Holdings, can extract gold, copper, silver, antimony and other minerals, including the rare earths necessary for myriad high-tech devices. One cell phone can yield up to 20 milligrams of gold; that may seem minuscule, but consider this: a ton of phones can provide 20 times more gold than a ton of gold ore.

The company's recycling process is based on methods long used by Dowa to get metals from raw ore. Disused, dismantled electronics are heated to 1,300 degrees Celsius, at which point 19 different metals (so far) can be extracted. It's working on ways to harvest more. One target: neodymium, a rare-earth essential for magnets used in everything from microphones to wind turbines.

Kosaka's eco-friendly innovation is well timed politically and economically. China, which mines about 93% of the world's rare-earth minerals, has slashed exports of them by 82% over the past year. For a period in late 2010, it cut off Japan's access to its rare earths entirely. "We are promoting the formation of a recycling-oriented society," Kosaka's website says – a modern take on the ancient Platonic observation that necessity is the mother of invention.'

Inspired leaders

Angela Ahrendts and Carlos Ghosn are no Mark Zuckerberg, yet they are reinventing age-old businesses through their personal passion for innovation. When asked about his impression of the all-electric Nissan Leaf, Ghosn's response was: 'It's fun to drive, but I can't describe it. The only way you'll discover it is by getting behind the wheel. There's no vibration, no smell, no noise. This is the future – and everything else is going to look obsolete, like sending messages with pigeons' (**www.fastcompany.com/most-innovative-companies/2011**).

Does this mean Ford and GM become messenger pigeons? Maybe not, but Nissan's wager is on the table. Innovative companies and their leaders cannot help but be radical.

Huawei's CEO Ren Zhengfei has just under half his staff working in R&D and, not surprisingly, while the rest of the world focuses on the possibilities of monetizing 3G and 4G mobile networks, Zhengfei has '100G' on his purpose list.

In 10 years' time, it could be Fast Company's 'The world's most innovative companies' (or some similar) list that helps form public opinion on which organizations – and their purposeful leaders – are the best and brightest. Quite like the 'Fortune 500' faithfully tracked the high impact of the leadership of Weill, Sloan or Welch over the last 55 years. Yet, in the age of persistent innovation, 10 years is a lifetime. Of the 50 companies on Fast Company's 2010 list 74 per cent fell off within a year. That's the new velocity of ideas.

Talent economics

03

Innovative solutions to new challenges seldom come from familiar places. GYAN NAGPAL

A competition of equals

Most middle-aged tennis fans have a date – 5 July 1980 – etched in memory. On that day a few thousand lucky people seated around centre court in Wimbledon, and many more watching on the TV – including Nelson Mandela interned on Robben Island, and I, an impressionable young man glued to a small black and white TV – got to witness our slice of sporting history. Bjorn Borg, the odds-on favourite of both bookmakers and the crowd, took on the impertinent genius of John McEnroe in what many consider the greatest Grand Slam final in the history of tennis. A tense five-set thriller, with more twists than Chubby Checker in his prime, the match reached an unbearable climax in the fourth set when McEnroe denied Borg no less than five championship points to eventually win the fourth set 18–16 in the tie-break. A Borg fan, I was broken. I also knew that the fourth would prove more than just a set. It was a mental and emotional test that gave its victor, in this case McEnroe, a psychological trump card. Borg, at the other end, looked broken too. Few gave the Swede any chance of recovering his composure in the fifth. But Bjorn Borg, called the ice man for ample reason, not only held his nerve but incredibly raised his game to win the deciding set 8–6, and with it a fifth consecutive Wimbledon title.

In marked contrast, many years later, I watched Pete Sampras demolish Cédric Pioline in probably the most boring and one-sided final in Wimbledon history. Over in a bare 90 minutes, I would not go so far as to call it a contest.

There is something about a competition of equals that takes the game to a completely new level. Although loaded with risks and pressure, a playing field where everyone has a fair opportunity to win, makes winners play beyond themselves, and over time improves the game as a whole.

As we sketched out in Chapter 1, the global economy is in similar circumstances today. The world before 1989 was a disconnected duopoly where competing political ideology divided much of mankind into opposing capitalist and socialist camps. Since 1990, the global economy has become inextricably conjoined, with technology and capital flows accelerating the creation of a universal playing field. And new players have emerged, in unexpected clusters, with similar trajectories and brand new game plans.

The heavyweight has new challengers

Global competition today doesn't resemble anything we have seen in recent history and, as a result, we cannot find recourse in a familiar set of rules. In reality, the game itself is changing, unwinding the very rules that have guided business for centuries. So much so, that the match between the prosperous and the aspirants, is increasingly beginning to resemble a competition of equals.

On one side you have the reigning heavyweight economic block, the Organisation for Economic Co-operation and Development (OECD). Made up of 34 countries comprising the 'open economies' of the developed world, the OECD has enjoyed economic supremacy as the primary player post the Cold War. OECD countries believe in the open market economic system, where the state has minimal involvement in the economy.

Staring down the heavyweight, in the other corner, we have the challengers. In 2000 investment banking firm Goldman Sachs clustered four of the hottest growth economies together and called them the 'BRIC countries'. Since then the high growth and high potential economies of Brazil, Russia, India and China have emerged as players of equal stature to the OECD. In the 10 years since 2000, the BRIC economies grew by 297 per cent compared to global growth of just 32 per cent. Projections state this gulf in economic growth is set to persist. But growth is always relative, and many citizens in the BRIC countries are poor, and huge social challenges like a lack of basic amenities and chronic illiteracy must be overcome before these countries achieve their full potential. Yet the countries themselves are not poor. As Mark Deen of the *Financial Times* noted in an article 'The West's share of global GDP set to fall' (3 June 2009), today, with roughly 40 per cent of the world's population, the BRIC collectively control 41 per cent of the world's foreign exchange reserves.

More recently, in 2009, the acronym CIVETS was coined by Robert Ward, Global Forecasting Director for the Economist Intelligence Unit (see the article 'The World in 2010', *The Economist* blogs, posted on 26 November 2009). Set to signify the next big opportunities in the developing world , CIVETS – which is also the name of the small tree-dwelling cat-like mammals found in Asia and Africa – stands for the dynamic and high potential economies of Colombia, Indonesia, Vietnam, Egypt, Turkey and South Africa. Whether the CIVETS group becomes the next big thing is yet to be seen, but one thing is certain – as economic power gets more widely distributed, the competition is going to be intense, for capital, for resources and for world-class talent.

The need for a strategic shift

As the operative players, the OECD, BRIC and CIVETS countries represent a broader shift in the global landscape. We are entering a new era of economic 'multi-polarity' and the implications for globally connected businesses are immense.

Let's exemplify this from the perspective of a large global company. If I was CEO of one of the world's 2,000 largest companies, let's say a member of the Forbes 2,000 club, I'd have a 7 in 10 chance of having headquarters in one of the 34 OECD countries. If I was CEO of one of those seven companies I would most likely have been born and raised surrounded by free-market thinking, and found it relatively easy to grow in countries that shared my business ideologies.

Now link what we have read above to what we discussed in Chapter 1: 'companies seeking to be truly global in 2020 will have no option but to be domestically relevant in both developed and emerging economies'. With the growth in emerging economies forecasted at double (and in some cases triple) the number in the developed world, many of the world's largest companies today are investing heavily in the emerging world. But what many are realizing is that this expansion isn't as synchronous and predictable as they would like. Mindsets differ, as do business practices. There is less transparency and greater governmental interference. There is less freedom and more procedure.

Faced with no other alternative than to dive in head first, many global businesses are painfully realizing that their franchises in the developing world require fundamental flexibility in both style of management and mix of talent. In the emerging world, each country's rule book is different, making centralized global strategy a hazardous gamble to execute. As investments into these markets grow, strategists are progressively waking up to the need for a strong and autonomous local strategy – one that is different for each country and uniquely tailored to local conditions. They are waking up to the central paradox of 21st-century business. **The only way to control chaos and complexity is to give up some of that control.** Organizations need to embed teams locally, build local partnerships, hire different skills and decentralize more.

Figure 3.1 shows results from the McKinsey Global Survey 'Five forces reshaping the global economy' (McKinsey & Company, 2010) and provides some evidence of the spectrum of strategies commonly employed by businesses pursuing global expansion or growth. The two most popular strategies for emerging market growth seem to be building greater captive local presence, and using the joint venture or partnership approach to build local presence. The implications on talent management are huge, as the respondents tell us. Of these, 47 per cent are actively recruiting talent from emerging markets and 42 per cent are deploying talent from more advanced markets to emerging markets to aid growth

A deciding factor of success in the global marketplace will be an organization's skill at managing the diversity of its human resource. Yet our ability to manage 'global talent' hasn't evolved at the same pace as our business footprint. How many times have we seen an organization make strategic decisions to invest millions of dollars in a new market or industry first, and months later look at key talent

FIGURE 3.1   Growth in emerging markets

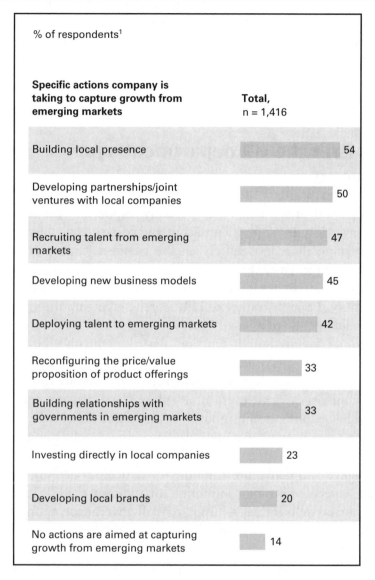

% of respondents[1]

Specific actions company is taking to capture growth from emerging markets	Total, n = 1,416
Building local presence	54
Developing partnerships/joint ventures with local companies	50
Recruiting talent from emerging markets	47
Developing new business models	45
Deploying talent to emerging markets	42
Reconfiguring the price/value proposition of product offerings	33
Building relationships with governments in emerging markets	33
Investing directly in local companies	23
Developing local brands	20
No actions are aimed at capturing growth from emerging markets	14

SOURCE: McKinsey & Company (2010) McKinsey Global Survey 'Five forces reshaping the global economy'.

metrics such as supply of engineers, graduate education numbers or workforce demographics as an afterthought? Many of these considerations probably only emerge during implementation, when an acute shortage of talent can be felt on the ground. In practice, because of insufficient or poor quality HR forecasting, many companies end up missing performance deadlines or having to rely on expensive expatriations to plug critical capability gaps.

There are two solutions to this problem. First, include strong talent analytics and talent strategy formulation in the strategic business planning cycle and, second, don't delegate this to the HR department.

This isn't the HR department's job, it's yours

Managing talent is a line manager's daily responsibility and, by that same yardstick, developing a proactive and commercial talent strategy is something that sits squarely on the business leader's table. The best leaders recognize this, and count it among their most important responsibilities. Other leaders chose to give this away, delegating the leadership of talent strategy to HR, thereby giving up the very cards that could help them win.

I am not saying the HR function mustn't be involved. Indeed the HR department has a very important role to play – a contributory and facilitative one. It has access to huge mountains of employee data, controls critical levers of employee engagement and hence should have an important input to strategy. But the HR department shouldn't be the one deciding or driving strategic talent imperatives. As a technical function it sits on the periphery, providing advice, governance and delivering a number of critical services to keep the people aspects of business in motion. In addition, the HR function's fundamental deliverables – hiring, payroll governance, training, employee information, talent mobility, etc – make it process-centric to begin with.

As a direct result, it is easy to spot HR-anchored talent strategy. First, it will be full of HR processes – performance and talent management practices, training programmes, incentive schemes, assessment centres and the like. Second, the strategy often needs to be sold to a room full of business leaders who agree, but don't know how to participate in intricate HR craft. In doing so, we lose the two most important ingredients of successful talent strategy – leadership accountability and broad-based participation.

Clear the ownership confusion

The first step for us is to clear up the confusion over roles and responsibilities. Leaders own, the HR department supports. A symptom of confusion can be seen from the responses of this survey (McKinsey & Company, 2008), which tells us that 75 per cent of HR professionals feel that HR has the capabilities to develop talent strategies aligned to business plans, yet close to 6 out of 10 managers disagree.

FIGURE 3.2   The perception gap

	% of interviewees in each category who agree	Gap, percentage points
● Human-resources (HR) professionals ● Line managers	0 25 50 75 100	
HR lacks capabilities to develop talent strategies aligned with business objectives	25 ● ● 58	33
HR is administrative department, not strategic business partner	51 ● ● 60	9
HR relies too much on best practices – some of which are inappropriate – when designing systems	30 ● 38	8
HR is not held accountable for success or failure of talent-management initiatives	36 ● ● 64	28
HR lacks authority/respect to influence the way people are managed	38 ● 47	9
Talent management is viewed as responsibility of HR	36 ● ● 58	22
HR doesn't provide enough support to line managers	43 ● ● 58	15

SOURCE: McKinsey & Company (2008) 'Making talent a strategic priority', *McKinsey Quarterly*.

It is clear that the HR function currently isn't helping its own cause. By pitching someone else's best practice, programmes, initiatives and 'tweaking' existing processes in the name of strategy, it is distracting leadership focus from a greater goal – commercial talent strategy that is embedded at the very core of business strategy.

Talent economics offers a fresh perspective

The truth is that many business leaders and HR professional are stuck and need a renewed perspective on what talent strategy in the 21st century could look like. The last two chapters of this book aim to address that. Our aim is make the talent strategy conversation much more intuitive, commercial and easily understood by line managers. This is where economics can be invaluable to talent management as a disciple – because at its heart economics is the study of how the forces of demand and supply allocate scarce resources.

As we have already seen, talent today is an increasingly fluid resource that is subject to the same laws of demand and supply as other precious commodities. In addition, shifts in employment loyalty have hastened the commoditization of talent. Going forward, traditional HR models and practices may prove inadequate in their ability to analyse and manage this resource. I have found that using economic constructs and techniques can help achieve breakthrough approaches in talent analytics and management.

Interdisciplinary thinking

Economics as a science has been around for centuries, whereas the first concepts on scientifically managing and motivating people at the workplace emerged in the early 20th century. A number of economic practices, such as splitting out macroeconomic factors, which focus on an economy, industry or society as a whole, from microeconomics, which is more concerned with the behaviour of individual players in a system, can be used to improve our analysis of an organization's talent imperatives.

Talent economics hence lives at the fulcrum of talent management and economic analysis, and is a natural response to the complexities of global business today. As more and more companies expand their footprint globally, and compete for talent in complex international markets, economic analysis of talent trends associates well with other economic factors that have an impact on business strategy. But we aren't doing anything new: interdisciplinary experimentation isn't a new practice, it has been around for ages. So much so that the best example is 500 years old and comes from Florence, Italy.

The Renaissance

In medieval Europe, just after the period known as the Dark Ages, came an era of intense artistic achievement. It started in a specific place, at a specific time and ostensibly came out of nowhere – a fact that confounded historians of that era. It was in Florence during the 14th century that cultural enquiry and artistic creativity suddenly spiked. And it wasn't just one art that flourished, or two, but a confluence of various disciplines – painters, writers and sculptors started creating masterpieces in parallel. The Renaissance was undoubtedly one of greatest creative phases of human history.

Within a short 50 years, Florence came to be known as the city of learning and a magnet for creative talent from across Europe. Great artists, scientists, writers, philosophers, sculptors and architects came together to pool knowledge and collectively resurrect creative thought from the confines of religion.

Artistic masterpieces such as 'The Birth of Venus' (Botticelli), 'The Madonna and the Child' (Filippo Lippi), 'The Last Supper' and 'The Mona Lisa' (Leonardo da Vinci) were created. Architects built some of the biggest and most intricate domes and palaces (Filippo Brunelleschi), new thinking emerged about the universe (Galileo Galilei), anatomy (da Vinci) and other physical sciences. The first book on leadership, Machiavelli's *The Prince*, was also published around this time.

Invention had broken free. Brunelleschi, Donatello, Masaccio, Galileo, da Vinci, Machiavelli, Botticelli, Michelangelo, Raphael. There were geniuses at work – concurrently. And then, by the early 1600s, this intense chapter of creative brilliance tapered off and died.

Many historians have tried to recreate the factors that led to the Renaissance, the specific time of its birth and the reason for its sad demise. And the answer most often comes down to the influence of one family: the Medici.

One of the richest and most powerful families in Europe at the time, it was the early Medici's obsession with knowledge that created the unique circumstances for the birth of the Renaissance in Florence. In particular, it was Giovanni de' Medici, followed by his son Cosimo and great-grandson Lorenzo, who began funding a variety of artistic endeavours and scientific studies in the city of Florence. The Medici commissioned some of the greatest thinkers in Europe to gather in Florence and produce works of genius. Their efforts in supporting artists, in many cases for years on end while they studied, allowed these artists to experiment at the thresholds of their capability, and then push beyond it. In most cases, this led to some of the greatest masterpieces ever known to man. In addition to supporting artists and commissioning artworks, what Medici patronage allowed was interdisciplinary collaboration.

Artists from different genres began to intermingle and learn from each other. Architects influenced painters to paint in three dimensions; painters influenced the quality of fine detail in sculpture and so on. Even today, innovation as a consequence of two disconnected disciplines coming together to push each other's boundaries is called the Medici effect. Evidence of the Medici effect and its influence on innovation is so dramatic that with political upheaval in the 1600s, when the Medici family declined in power, so did the Renaissance.

Breakthrough innovation occurs when we bring down boundaries and encourage disciplines to learn from each other. The Medici were catalysts of innovation, and so powerful was their impact that, centuries later, their influence can still be felt. As we look at talent strategy for 21st-century organizations, there is much we can learn from the Renaissance.

Macro talent economics
The study of aggregate talent

04

'*Details create the big picture.*' SANFORD I WEILL

The big picture puts challenges in perspective

'*When we are no longer able to change a situation,*
we are challenged to change ourselves.' VIKTOR E FRANKL

Economic analysis must start with the big picture, with an attempt to see how conditions for business exist within an economic system in general. In the same vein, talent economics must begin by focusing on the labour force within a social system, be it a country, industry or job family globally. I recommend business leaders begin by identifying the macro talent trends swirling around them. By understanding changing workforce demographics, mobility trends or the student pipeline, business leaders start understanding the rules that govern the game.

Talent strategy that doesn't start with a macro view risks missing the wood for the trees, or assuming external factors are in alignment with internal goals. These are mistakes that could prove costly in the long run. A recent example is set out below.

CASE STUDY   A banking operation in China

While conducting a series of macro diagnosis interviews, I was recently introduced to Lars, a senior leader of a global financial major in Shanghai. Tasked with aggressive multi-year growth targets for the fledging banking operation he led in China, it was immediately clear to me that Lars was distracted and seemed to be agonizing about something. Considered a high performer all through his stellar career, back at headquarters Lars was seen as a 'young turk' – a change leader with immense credibility to see through tough projects. Yet, in recent months he had started doubting his own ability to make this assignment a success.

Three questions into our conversation, I felt I was leading a coaching session rather than a hard facts discussion on business data, for every query I made brought us back to the subject of escalating costs, specifically the cost of operation, the cost of talent and the cost of incubating the business in difficult competitive circumstances. Core to the issue Lars grappled with on a daily basis was the fact that his 'cost per transaction' was three times (if not more) that of his local competitors. As a consequence, he was doomed to report an operating loss quarter after quarter in spite of having every other business metric (network expansion, net new clients and quality of loans) tracking targets. 'My people costs are killing me,' he said, 'and everything we try seems to make the problem worse. I have to fix my escalating people cost curve, Gyan, or we risk HQ holding back the capital I desperately need to grow the business.'

Digging deeper into his talent issues, it was clear that Lars and his management team were choosing to react to the environment rather than create it. It was also clear the bank had not thought through its requirements for capability in several key roles, such as branch managers or risk analysts, and hence several times a month fell into two familiar traps.

The first was paying above the market to hire from the competition. Apart from driving up costs, this was proving a high-stakes gamble in a hot talent market like China. Money as a differentiator was buying the bank transient loyalty, with several of its hires leaving within a year or two, trading up to the next bidder.

The second error was using expatriations to fill junior talent gaps. Expatriation in itself isn't an uncommon strategy for young subsidiary organizations, and indeed could be strategically advantageous when used well, but every expatriate comes at a significant price premium and carries considerable success risk. Sure, requesting assignees from its headquarters for junior roles got the bank someone who had done the job before, but once the expenses were factored in, each expatriation cost four times what a local employee would. Further, with the business context between China and Europe being so different, Lars felt that barely half the assignees were adding value.

Avoiding the talent trap

Symptomatically, it looks as if Lars was caught in a talent trap. Rather than being an enabler of business, his talent challenges were slowing down business success. To use an analogy from chess, it's like finding your king trapped in a corner, battling for survival with fewer and fewer options to choose from. Lars felt he had lost the option to be proactive, and his only option was to react. And that's an issue. Trying not to lose isn't a substitute for playing to win.

A talent trap is a consequence often brought on by one of two causes. There is either a total absence of a market calibrated talent strategy. Or there is a strategy misfit, ie using strategy imported from elsewhere.

It's also quite seductive to attribute Lar's challenges to China as a market, where in the short run, China's local talent pool struggles to keep up with a red-hot economy. Yet China isn't the exception it is often positioned to be. Similar management risks exist in any high-context market across the world, be it South Africa, Hong Kong, Bolivia, Brazil or Vietnam. Each of these countries possesses differentiated talent marketplaces and hence warrants distinctive strategy.

Macro talent economics is the study of talent within a market system. As an input into strategy, it ensures that we map a country's workforce by analysing the variables that have an impact on local employment conditions. By studying trends we look to predict overall talent flows, availability of management talent, skills, employment proficiency and a host of other conditions that could have an impact on our organization's people strategy and practices.

A company that operates in one market alone would probably be intuitively aware of these trends and, as a result, find macro analysis relatively simple. But if the singular market is sufficiently large, such as the United States, China or India, the circumstances in one part of the country may be very different from another. It then becomes imperative to identify macro talent flows for each province or state where the company hires manpower. In India, for example, education quality can vary immensely from one state to another. While the country does have a common examination standard, 'employability' varies immensely depending on non-theoretical factors embedded in the education experience. The textbooks may be the same, but the quality of instruction differs immensely from one town to another. A suitably qualified customer service professional in Kochi in South India could be at a very different skill level compared to someone who has studied in Bhubaneswar on the east coast, or for that matter Mumbai on the west.

Every explorer needs a map and compass

The study of macro variables becomes absolutely critical when a company operates across multiple countries or in an international setting. In an increasingly connected world, more and more companies are expanding to new regions, adding new markets and acquiring operations in distant corners of the world. Understanding macro trends adds context to a number of people decisions and helps managers deal with both similarities and differences inherent in an unfamiliar 'talent system'. In practice, it can help managers avoid traps like the one Lars found himself in last year.

For the purpose of this book, we will study eight such macro talent factors that have a deep correlation to successful talent strategy. These eight aren't exclusive, and constitute at best the minimum insight needed into a talent system as a whole. Clubbed with micro factors covered in following chapters, they form a highly effective set of inputs for a world-class talent strategy.

I recommend macro talent analysis always start with the study of three simple 'quantitative' ratios that collectively establish the labour supply for a country in question. These are:

1 **Aggregate talent** – the study of workforce changes in an economy.

2 **Replacement and mobility ratios** – which reflect birth rates and migration trends within an economy. In other words, how many workers enter the labour force for every retirement?

3 **Age and dependency ratios** – which seek to identify how much employable talent exists in relation to those who are unemployable. In simple terms, how many dependents does an average worker support, and is this number increasing or decreasing? Age is another important perspective.

What are a country's age forecasts telling us, and how will this have an impact on labour supply or employment conditions?

Once these three ratios are established, we move on to demographic ratios and an analysis of the workforce mix. There are two distinct demographic perspectives:

4 The workforce's gender mix – average economic participation rates for women versus men, at all levels of the labour force, with a particular emphasis on women at various layers of management.

5 Generational shifts – generational markers for the countries in question and the implications of these on employment preferences and practices.

And finally, we can analyse three 'qualitative' macro variables critical to business:

6 Basic proficiency – the quality of basic education available and the impact it has on workforce proficiency levels.

7 Management proficiency – the quality of tertiary education experiences and the supply of future managers within a economy.

FIGURE 4.1 Macro talent pyramid

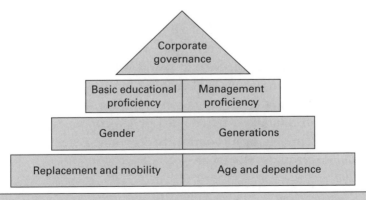

8 Governance and sustainability – the importance given to good governance and the ever-increasing focus on long-term sustainability within a social system.

Why are these eight insights – as illustrated in Figure 4.1 – important? Let's assume a company has capital invested in 15 countries worldwide and, as a result, runs individual country operations drawing from 15 distinctive talent markets. This company would be well served by macro trend analysis. Examining similarities and differences between these markets could help inform strategic talent investments for both the short and long term.

Aggregate global talent

When Neil Armstrong took man's first step on the moon on 21 July 1969, he did so as a representative of 3.6 billion other humans on planet earth. More recently, the popular press has been awash with China's publicly stated goal to send man back to the moon by 2020. If a Chinese astronaut does end up achieving this, he or she would be there representing more than twice the 1969 number of humans. By 2014 the world population will top 7.2 billion. Here's an illustration of how staggering this growth has been. It took 500,000 years since the first *Homo sapiens* existed, to grow the population to 3.6 billion. We then doubled that number in fewer than 50.

The past 60 years

Global population at the end of 2011 was a shade over 7 billion, a growth of 174 per cent over 1950, when the cycle of economic expansion started after the Second World War. Aggregate population growth forms an important backdrop for business, as it reflects both the labour pool and the per capita consumptions shifts in an economy. To get the ball rolling, we tested a list of 45 economies (listed in the box below), representing all continents, economic systems, population sizes and stages of development.

Argentina, Australia, Austria, Bangladesh, Bolivia, Botswana, Brazil, Canada, China, China-Hong Kong SAR, Colombia, Egypt, France, Germany, Guatemala, India, Indonesia, Iraq, Italy, Japan, Kenya, Malaysia, Mexico, Nigeria, Norway, Pakistan, Peru, Philippines, Poland, Portugal, Republic of Korea, Russian Federation, Singapore, South Africa, Spain, Sudan, Sweden, Switzerland, Thailand, Turkey, Ukraine, United Arab Emirates (UAE), United Kingdom, United States of America, Vietnam

We were looking for hotspots of population growth over the last 60 years. Table 4.1 (United Nations, 2011) shows what we found.

While China and India have always been the largest, what the UAE has done is nothing short of spectacular. When oil was first discovered there in the 1950s, the population of barely 70,000 consisted of mainly nomadic Bedouin tribes and fishermen. Since then the population has grown an incredible 100 times its 1950 base. Today, over 90 per cent of Dubai's workforce comes from overseas. Fuelled by the oil boom, UAE's GDP during the same period grew over 200 times (Maddison, 2007).

This spectacular growth is also possible without the blessing of large oil reserves, as Singapore and Hong Kong show us. Both locations figure in the top 20 and have strikingly similar economic personalities – they are equally small, lacking in valuable natural resources and ambitious. By becoming trading hubs, promoting good governance and investing in raising standards of living, both became incredibly attractive locations for migrant labour. As proof, while Singapore's population has grown fourfold in the last 60 years, the country's GDP has increased an incredible 100 times.

Unlocking the value of natural resources and increasing the quantity and quality of economic activity are the two strongest growth levers countries have today. More production and more consumption kick-start a virtuous cycle of growth and prosperity, better education, improved health and an increased standard of living for all. To do this, countries need to develop their labour forces on two fronts – capability and productivity.

TABLE 4.1   Population growth 1950–2010

Rank	Country	1950	2010	Growth %
1	United Arab Emirates	70	7 512	10 694.36
2	Kenya	6 077	40 513	566.68
3	Iraq	5 719	31 672	453.78
4	Philippines	18 397	93 261	406.95
5	Singapore	1 022	5 086	397.64
6	Botswana	413	2 007	386.49
7	Sudan	9 190	43 552	373.91
8	Malaysia	6 110	28 401	364.84
9	Pakistan	37 542	173 593	362.39
10	Guatemala	3 146	14 389	357.36
11	Nigeria	37 860	158 423	318.45
12	Mexico	27 866	113 423	307.03
13	Bangladesh	37 895	148 692	292.38
14	Colombia	12 000	46 295	285.80
15	Peru	7 632	29 077	280.96
16	Egypt	21 514	81 121	277.06
17	South Africa	13 683	50 133	266.38
18	Bolivia (Plurinational State of)	2 714	9 930	265.92
19	Brazil	53 975	194 946	261.18
20	China, Hong Kong SAR	1 974	7 053	257.30
	Selected lower ranks			
23	India	371 857	1 224 614	229.32
29	China	550 771	1 341 335	143.54
30	United States of America	157 813	310 384	96.68
34	Japan	82 199	126 536	53.94
41	United Kingdom	50 616	62 036	22.56
44	Germany	68 376	82 302	20.37
	WORLD Average	***2 532 229***	***6 895 889***	***172.32***

NOTE: All figures in thousands.
Source: United Nations, Department of Economic and Social Affairs, Population Division (2011) *World Population Prospects: The 2010 Revision*, CD-ROM edition.

The next 40 years

Looking forward, the hotspots of population shifts look quite different. Based on United Nations population projections (and assuming migration trends continue at current levels), Table 4.2 analyses population projections over the next 40 years for the same list of 45 representative economies given in the box on page 54.

TABLE 4.2   Population growth projections 2010–2050

Rank	Country	2010	2050	Growth %
1	Iraq	31 672	83 357	163.19
2	Nigeria	158 423	389 615	145.93
3	Kenya	40 513	96 887	139.15
4	Guatemala	14 389	31 595	119.58
5	Sudan	43 552	90 962	108.86
6	Bolivia	9 930	16 769	68.88
7	Philippines	93 261	154 939	66.13
8	United Arab Emirates	7 512	12 152	61.78
9	Pakistan	173 593	274 875	58.34
10	Malaysia	28 401	43 455	53.00
11	Egypt	81 121	123 452	52.18
12	Australia	22 268	31 385	40.94
13	India	1 224 614	1 692 008	38.17
	WORLD Average	6 895 889	9 306 128	34.95
14	Peru	29 077	38 832	33.55
15	Colombia	46 295	61 764	33.42
16	China, Hong Kong SAR	7 053	9 305	31.93
17	Bangladesh	148 692	194 353	30.71
18	United States of America	310 384	403 101	29.87
19	Canada	34 017	43 642	28.29
20	Mexico	113 423	143 925	26.89

TABLE 4.2 *Continued*

Rank	Country	2010	2050	Growth %
Selected lower ranks				
21	Turkey	72 752	91 617	25.93
26	Singapore	5 086	6 106	20.04
27	Vietnam	87 848	103 962	18.34
28	United Kingdom	62 036	72 817	17.38
31	Brazil	194 946	222 843	14.31
32	South Africa	50 133	56 757	13.21
37	Italy	60 551	59 158	−2.30
38	Republic of Korea	48 184	47 050	−2.35
39	China	1 341 335	1 295 604	−3.41
41	Germany	82 302	74 781	−9.14
42	Russian Federation	142 958	126 188	−11.73
44	Japan	126 536	108 549	−14.22
45	Ukraine	45 448	36 074	−20.63

NOTE: All figures in thousands.
SOURCE: United Nations, Department of Economic and Social Affairs, Population Division (2011) (medium fertility variant) *World Population Prospects: The 2010 Revision*, CD-ROM edition.

An African sunrise

The popular perception out there is that Asia is the global engine of population growth. This is true when you look at absolute numbers. After all, the two most populous countries in the world come from one neighbourhood. However, when you look at relative growth rates across continents over a 100-year period, from 1950 to 2050, the graph looks something like the one shown in Figure 4.2.

Over this century, Asia barely tracks the global averages. The African labour force, currently devastated by the HIV epidemic and home to some of poorest countries in the world, will grow over eight times its 1950 numbers. Latin America follows next, with the developed continents predictably at the bottom. The question every business leader must ask before investing millions of dollars in

FIGURE 4.2 100-year projections by region (1950–2050)

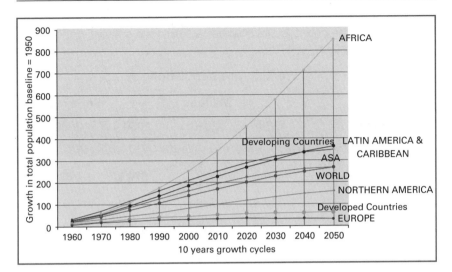

SOURCE: United Nations, Department of Economic and Social Affairs, Population Division (2011) (Medium fertility variant) *World Population Prospects: The 2010 Revision*, CD-ROM edition

far-flung international markets is: how will this have an impact on my business?

The global workforce

Aggregate population numbers provide a contextual underlay to changes in a country's workforce over time. From a strategy perspective, it would serve us better to strip out from the total population numbers those who are too young to work and those beyond the retirement age. The residual number is a much better data point for business.

Table 4.3 shows data from the Stanford Center on Longevity (a think-tank focused on the impact of ageing on populations). It profiles the 15 largest workforces in the world today and what they could look like in 2050.

Economic juggernauts such as Japan, Russia, Germany and China will all face a potential workforce contraction over the next 40 years, bought on primarily by historically low birth rates. Many emerging markets too have seen birth rates slide. But with relatively younger

TABLE 4.3   The 15 largest workforces

Several large countries (in bold below) will face smaller world forces by 2050.

Working-age population

| Country | Millions | | | Indexed |
	1950	2010	2050	2050 / 2010
1. China	**337.8**	**973.3**	**870.1**	**0.89**
2. India	220.8	780.6	1,098.0	1.41
3. United States	102.2	212.3	247.9	1.17
4. Indonesia	43.9	156.4	184.3	1.18
5. Brazil	29.9	132.2	137.2	1.04
6. Pakistan	23.8	109.6	224.1	2.04
7. Bangladesh	25.2	107.2	148.8	1.39
8. Russia	**66.7**	**101.2**	**70.1**	**0.69**
9. Nigeria	20.3	86.3	192.2	2.23
10. Japan	**49.4**	**81.6**	**51.8**	**0.63**
11. Mexico	15.0	72.5	79.5	1.10
12. Vietnam	17.5	61.1	70.6	1.16
13. Philippines	10.6	58.3	96.8	1.66
14. Germany	**45.9**	**54.3**	**38.7**	**0.71**
15. Iran	9.4	53.6	61.3	1.14
EU 27	**246.4**	**333.4**	**279.8**	**0.84**
World	1,536.0	4,523.7	5,865.8	1.30

SOURCE: Stanford Center on Longevity/Hayutin, A (2010) Population age shifts will reshape global workforce; United Nations (medium variant forecast) *World Population Prospects, The 2008 Revision*.
NOTE: Working age is defined here as 15–64 years old.

populations, emerging markets will continue to grow their labour pool, although the pace of growth will eventually slow. This growth, along with improved healthcare and education in many disadvantaged nations, will result in the global workforce growing by one third between now and 2050.

Hayutin, the author of the workforce study shown in Table 4.3, also makes an important observation on her forecast: 'Potential work-force size could be further expanded by increasing workforce participation rates at the traditional working ages or by expanding the definition of working age to include older workers' (Hayutin, 2010).

Beyond winning and losing, it's participation that counts

Increasing participation rates is an important way of supplementing a country's labour force, but participation means different things in mature economies than in the developing world. For example, after the 2008–09 financial crisis many mature economies saw large swaths of redundant workers struggling to find suitable re-employment, and as a result choosing to drop out of the labour market and stay unemployed. By doing this they not only risk redundancy of current knowledge and skills, they risk losing out to technology shifts and being eventually replaced by a younger or cheaper workforce. After the crisis, we have also seen part-time employment increasing sharply, further reducing workforce participation rates. The International Labour Organization (ILO) estimates that between 2007 and 2010, 55 per cent of the global increase in unemployment happened in developed economies and the EU region (ILO, 2011). This cluster of countries accounts for just 15 per cent of the world's population. In regions such as the Middle East, a combination of high unemployment and little or no social support has ravaged the work climate and led to significant social unrest. The Middle East currently has the highest unemployment rate in the world. Hidden within the 10 per cent overall regional unemployment rate is the sad state of youth joblessness, which is almost four times the adult rate (ILO, 2011).

In the emerging markets, the challenges of increasing workforce participation are quite different. Primary among them is the access to early education, without which a large percentage of youth have no access to better quality jobs. Social inequity is another challenge, which denies women and other demographics equal opportunities.

A choice we made

Putting off retirement can be another way of increasing workforce participation. As we discussed in Chapter 1, the concept of retirement is getting less and less defined, and a lot of workers are continuing to work beyond traditional retirement age. As life expectancy increases, working longer is beneficial to the economy too. It helps ease the burden on social support and state sponsored healthcare. Today many choose to continue working because of personal circumstances or simply choice. We will see later in this chapter, when we discuss ageing and dependency ratios, that in many economies by 2020 the elderly will no longer have this choice. Age-defined retirement will come to be viewed as a luxury, and most will be expected to work as long as their health permits. Yet paradoxically, this is also a choice we made – by opting to have fewer children.

The fertility factor

My grandmother is one of seven children; and before her 21st birthday she had produced four of her own. Each of her four children grew up to have either one or two children. The deeply loved matriarch of our family often recounts how in the society of her time children were a sign of prosperity. But even in our microcosm family that view has turned on its head, and birth rates have halved with every generation. This phenomenon is playing out throughout the world too. In both developing and developed countries, birth rates today are at historic lows. With 7 billion people on the planet, this can be a good thing. It reduces strain on the environment, slows down resource utilization and with smaller numbers to contend with, governments have a better chance of improving services such as early healthcare and education for children. But in countries where the population is unable to 'replace' itself, this also has a deep implication on economic vibrancy and the very nature of the labour force.

A country's total fertility rate (TFR) indicates the average number of children born per woman during her lifetime. If a country has a fertility rate of 2.4, it means that, on average, there are 2.4 babies born per female resident during her lifetime. Yet this number in itself cannot predict changes in a country's long-term population numbers. In order to make medium- and long-term projections, we also need to know the replacement rate for the country in question. The replacement rate indicates a TFR number at which a population will remain constant over time. It factors in infant mortality, the impact of diseases and other social factors such as the gender ratio in the country. Based on data analysed over the most recent decade, most developed nations have a replacement ratio between 2.05 and 2.1. For emerging markets such as China and India, the replacement ratio is between 2.1 and 2.3; and in the least developed nations in the world such as Sierra Leone and Afghanistan, this number can go as high as 3.4 (Engelman and Leahy, 2006).

This book is about talent strategy in 2020, and how our approach to talent strategy will need to differ by country. It is therefore fairly easy to map the increases and decreases in a country's natural labour force over the current decade (2010–20) by analysing birth rates from 20 years ago.

Assuming factors such as migration remain constant, if birth rates stay above the replacement rate, we will have more 15–25-year-olds entering higher education and eventually the workforce than those attaining retirement ages. If birth rates are well below the replacement rate, we will have to contend with dwindling sources of fresh talent. Table 4.4 looks at the same sample set of 45 countries we examined earlier.

Young talent entering the workforce 2010–20

By analysing the total fertility rates (per female resident) between 1995 and 2005, it is fairly easy to predict how much young talent will be entering the workforce between now and 2020. In some places the pipeline of young employees will be robust; in others it will be bleak – priceless insight for any company investing millions of incremental dollars in a growing business. Table 4.4 represents total

TABLE 4.4   Fertility rates 1995–2005

Country/ Economy	1995–2000 TFR	2000–2005 TFR
Nigeria	6.05	5.67
Sudan	5.41	4.82
Kenya	5.07	5.00
Iraq	5.40	4.63
Guatemala	5.00	4.60
Pakistan	4.98	4.44
Bolivia	4.32	3.96
Botswana	3.70	3.18
Egypt	3.50	3.16
India	3.46	3.11
Bangladesh	3.30	2.80
Southern Africa	3.09	2.90
Malaysia	3.10	2.85
Peru	3.10	2.80
World average	*2.82*	*2.67*
United Arab Emirates	2.97	2.49
Colombia	2.75	2.55
Mexico	2.67	2.40
Argentina	2.63	2.35
Indonesia	2.55	2.38
Turkey	2.57	2.23
Vietnam	2.50	2.25
Brazil	2.45	2.25

TABLE 4.4 *Continued*

Country/ Economy	1995–2000 TFR	2000–2005 TFR
United States of America	1.99	2.04
Thailand	1.86	1.81
Norway	1.85	1.80
France	1.76	1.88
China	1.80	1.77
Australia	1.78	1.75
United Kingdom	1.70	1.70
Sweden	1.56	1.67
Canada	1.56	1.52
Singapore	1.57	1.36
Portugal	1.46	1.44
Switzerland	1.47	1.42
Austria	1.37	1.39
South Korea	1.51	1.22
Poland	1.48	1.25
Germany	1.34	1.35
Japan	1.37	1.30
Russia	1.25	1.30
Spain	1.18	1.29
Italy	1.22	1.26
Ukraine	1.23	1.15

SOURCE: United Nations, Department of Economic and Social Affairs, Population Division (2011) *World Population Prospects: The 2010 Revision.*

fertility rates between 1995 and 2005 in two progressive five-year blocks.

China's low numbers are particularly interesting, as are the shrinking numbers of new workers in red-hot economies such as Russia. Or for that matter compare the numbers for Thailand and Malaysia. These neighbours are promising locations for investment, yet have dramatically different demographic trends playing out locally.

The figures for several countries are well below the replacement rate, and while Japan and Western Europe get a lot of press on ageing populations, the situation is particularly grim in East Europe. As a case in point, let's study Russia for a moment.

The Russian replacement rate was a healthy 2.15 in the late 1980s, allowing its population to peak at a healthy 149 million by 1993. But dismantling the Soviet economic legacy was a very painful process for most Russians and, as a result, fertility dropped to 1.25 by the late 90s. While it has inched up slightly in recent times, the previous period of low fertility is working its way through the labour pool at the moment and the Russian economy will be challenged by dwindling supplies of young talent all through this decade.

In Asia, low fertility is a pressing concern all across the eastern half of the continent. South Korea is in particular trouble. With fertility at 1.2–1.3 for much of the last two decades, South Korea faces an acute talent crunch.

The Korean situation is a case of a government birth-control programme that worked too well for its own good. In fact, births in South Korea used to average over 6 children per woman in the late 1950s – a time when the country experienced a baby boom after the Korean War ended. In the 1960s and 1970s, the government, fearing their small country might get overcrowded, launched a family-planning programme, which ended up being so effective that the Korean TFR plummeted below 2 in the 1980s. Today Korea's TFR is one of the lowest in the world, and more and more Korean women are choosing careers over parenthood. Many are delaying marriage, or choosing not to get married at all, a social tilt that is proving hard to reverse. As a result, current estimates indicate that Korea will age rapidly by 2050, with 40 per cent of its population over the age of 65.

For countries with dwindling fertility, migration is probably the best policy response to augment talent in the medium term. Indeed, it will prove crucial for countries such as Singapore, Hong Kong, Germany and Japan as they negotiate the impact of their own dwindling supply of talent over the next 40 years. Today, 40 per cent of Singapore residents were born overseas. Even mid-sized populations such as those in Australia and Canada comprise over 20 per cent migrant stock. At the time of writing this book, the United States has over 42 million overseas-born residents.

Note: The talent economics toolkit at the end of this book includes a select list of data sources and research publications for those looking to deepen their understanding of aggregate talent trends.

An older and wiser world

Sliding fertility rates bring us to what is arguably the biggest challenge facing a number of global policy makers today – managing an ageing population. It is common knowledge that rapidly ageing nations across Europe and East Asia will face an economic speed breaker sometime over the next 25 years. Brought on by increases in life expectancy and the 'below replacement' birth rates we discussed earlier, this increase in average age does have a major impact on macro talent trends across the world.

Figure 4.3, sourced from the United Nations, demonstrates a 100-year trend line of shifting population numbers across three critical age bands:

- those below 15 years old (represented by the darkest shading);
- the bulk of the world's labour pool, made up of those between 15 and 59 (shown in medium shading);
- the global population over 60 (represented by the lightest shading).

As we can see, the world as a whole will age, brought on in equal measures by increases in life expectancy and a decline in birth rates (part A of Figure 4.3). This phenomenon isn't limited to a few countries or regions, but is broad based across a wide spectrum of developed and emerging markets (parts B and C).

FIGURE 4.3   Distribution of population by broad age groups: world and development regions, 1950–2050

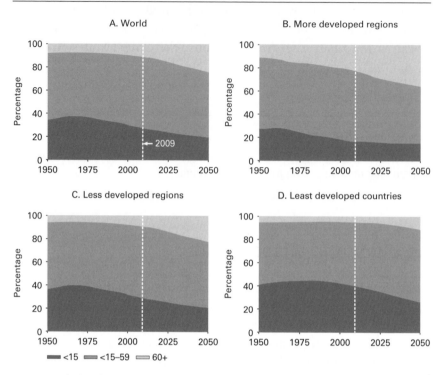

A. World

B. More developed regions

C. Less developed regions

D. Least developed countries

■ <15 ▬ <15–59 ▬ 60+

SOURCE: United Nations, Department of Economic and Social Affairs (2009) *World Population Ageing Report.*

Age issues of a different kind

Most of the world's least developed countries (part D), are clustered in sub-Saharan Africa, where the impact of AIDS and other diseases has a crippling effect on workforce demographics. The average age across sub-Saharan Africa in 2010 was a depressed 18.7 – more than 11 years younger than the world average. The impact of AIDS on overall life expectancy can also been seen from Figure 4.4. For a high potential emerging economy such as South Africa, the reduction in life expectancy due to AIDS is a staggering 13 years on average.

Yet concerted effort over the last 20 years on HIV prevention is finally bearing first fruits, with the latest data showing a slow decline in HIV transmission rates across sub-Saharan Africa. I am confident these improvements will continue, mainly through greater awareness

FIGURE 4.4 Life expectancy at birth in the 10 countries with the highest HIV prevalence compared with that from a no-AIDS scenario, 2005–2010

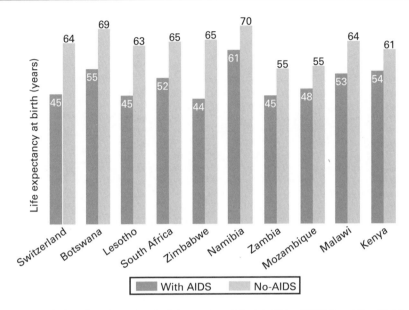

SOURCE: United Nations Department of Economic and Social Affairs (2010) Population Division, *Population and HIV/AIDS 2010*.

and support for those hardest hit. But even if Africa stages a miracle recovery, the ravaging effects of AIDS on the African workforce will take a further 40 years to work their way through the labour system.

Outside of Africa too, age has profound implications on long-term economics. Within the next decade, average ages in many countries will be on the higher side of 40. By 2020, the average age in China will be 38. India, on the other hand, will continue to be a relatively young country, with an average age of 28. This 10-year advantage will prove instrumental in sustaining India's talent pipeline during the 2030s and 2040s, a time when China will struggle in comparison.

Globally connected organizations will increasingly have to contend with the challenges age differences create for pay and benefit programmes, performance equity and mobility of talent. 2020 isn't far away, and in some sectors of the global economy age differences are already playing out. For example, many companies shipping manufacturing or services activities over to high-growth emerging markets face the situation described in the case study below.

TABLE 4.5   The 2020 world age profile

Country	Median age
WORLD Average	*31.6*
Japan	48.2
Germany	47.7
Italy	46.8
Hong Kong	45.3
Portugal	45.1
Austria	45.0
Switzerland	44.5
Greece	44.4
Spain	44.1
Netherlands	43.5
Croatia	43.5
Finland	43.0
South Korea	43.0
Singapore	42.7
Sweden	41.7
Canada	41.6
France	41.3
Poland	41.1
United Kingdom	40.4
Norway	40.4
Russia	39.8
Australia	38.2
Thailand	38.2
China	38.1
United States of America	37.9

TABLE 4.5 *Continued*

Country	Median age
United Arab Emirates	36.9
Brazil	33.4
Vietnam	33.1
Argentina	32.8
Turkey	32.1
Indonesia	31.4
Mexico	30.1
Colombia	30.0
Malaysia	28.9
India	28.1
Egypt	27.5
South Africa	27.1
Pakistan	24.7
Philippines	24.5
Bolivia	24.1
Ethiopia	21.8
Sudan	21.4
Iraq	19.8
Kenya	19.2
Nigeria	18.8
Tanzania	17.4
Mali	16.9
Malawi	16.6
Uganda	16.6
Niger	15.9

SOURCE: United Nations, Department of Economic and Social Affairs, Population Division (2011) (medium variant forecast), *World Population Prospects: The 2010 Revision*, CD-ROM edition.

CASE STUDY

A large financial services firm was well into a major migration of transaction processing work from its US operations over to an outsourced vendor in the Philippines. As we saw in Chapter 1, this is a very popular 'cost-play' strategy in global organizations today. By shipping off basic services to low-cost emerging markets, many companies are able to reflect large savings in overall cost. The majority of this saving comes from much lower labour cost, which in itself is influenced by a healthy supply of young talent lining up for jobs.

However, in this case, the migration of work to Manila was fraught with quality challenges, and many service levels were well below expectations. When we analysed the situation, the reason for poor quality was not capability, or motivation, or the quality of upfront staff training – which was in fact quite comprehensive.

The two major reasons were extremely high employee turnover levels at the junior levels and inexperienced management. In this case, very inexperienced. The average supervisor was 25 years old; the average middle manager was 29. Each middle manager managed an operation made up of several hundred employees.

The situation described in the case study isn't unfamiliar, and represents a common reconciliation required when moving work overseas, especially to a country with a vastly different workforce.

Working beyond retirement

At the other end of the spectrum, we have a wave of impending retirements in a number of developed economies. In the United States, the baby boomer generation is up for retirement and the lucky few will soon be cashing in their pensions. But for the majority retirement may actually mean 'back to work'. Many of them are eager to continue working, and yet more are forced to, due to the ravages of recent market volatility on their pension plans. Today, the economic impact of an ageing population is at the top of government agendas in many developed countries. It has an obvious and direct impact on social security schemes, government labour policy and industries such as healthcare, insurance and pension funds. The question we must ask though is whether changes in average age should matter to talent economists in the private sector. I feel they do.

Ageing does warrant much closer study in global organizations, more so because it has a tendency to creep up on policy, undetected. Indeed, even to the many government experts discussing the potential impact of ageing on employment policy, it still feels like something out there. Something on the horizon. And in putting it off as a future problem, they risk having to make a mad last-minute dash to catch a train that has already started moving.

One such example is retirement legislation. As *The Economist* comments on US retirement policy 'When America introduced its Social Security (public pension) scheme in 1935 to prevent poverty in old age, the retirement age was 65 and life expectancy at birth was 62. In 1983 a decision was made to raise the official retirement age to 67, but in steps so tiny that the move will not be completed until 2027. Life expectancy at birth in America now averages about 78...' (*The Economist*, 2009a).

By 2027, the US life expectancy at birth will be well over 80, yet the official retirement age will be 67. This doesn't necessarily mean people over the retirement age don't work. Indeed, with greater longevity and better healthcare, many are willing and able. Yet an official retirement age creates discriminatory societal influences that hinder employment for the elderly. Insurance companies, hiring managers and job agencies all get influenced.

The solution unfortunately isn't as easy as pushing the retirement age back a few more years: we need a whole new perspective on ageing. This must start from a more flexible policy on retirement age, and move to other easy to implement options like 'scale back' programmes for older employees that could allow those over 60 the option to choose less-demanding jobs, and flexi-work options such as job sharing or other part-time arrangements. Many older workers I have spoken to relish the idea of a partial retirement – such as working two or three days a week. With empty nests and lots of spare time, they are keen to contribute, but worry about the rigours of a five-day working week. A reduction in wages doesn't matter as much to them as continued medical cover and extra time for adequate rest and recovery.

An increasingly dependent world

Managing an ageing workforce will require subtly differentiated responses by country and region. A good indicator of the force ageing exerts on society as a whole can be seen from changes in dependency ratios over time. In economic terms, a '65+ dependency ratio' demonstrates the number of people 65 and over for every 100 people in the workforce (in this instance the workforce is defined as all individuals between 20 and 64).

The country with the highest old-age dependency ratio today is Japan, which has close to 40 people aged 65 and over for every 100 in their working prime. By 2020 this number will be at 52, and close to 70 by the year 2040.

Figure 4.5 profiles the old age dependency predictions for a number of countries and the four principal economic regions in the year 2020 and 2040.

FIGURE 4.5   Old age dependency ratios in 2010 and predictions for 2020 and 2040

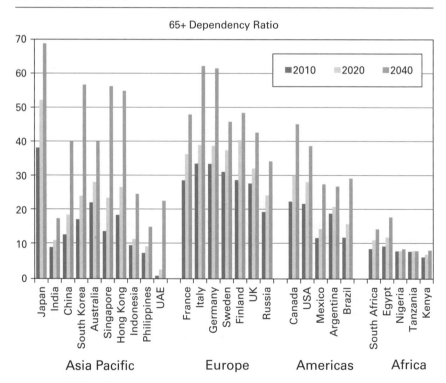

65+ Dependency Ratio

SOURCE: United Nations, Department of Economic and Social Affairs, Population Division (2011) (medium variant forecast), *World Population Prospects: The 2010 Revision*, CD-ROM edition

Increasing dependence, as we can see, is a worldwide phenomenon, affecting every region except Africa. Countries that don't focus on the economic contribution of their older populations risk exacerbating a shrinking talent pipeline, or driving up labour costs.

Organizations have a responsibility too. The logical first step for companies with operations in ageing economies is a thorough age analysis of their current employee populations. If the internal age profile doesn't mirror societal trends, the second step I recommend is an audit of internal practices and policies. Review your hiring practices, benefit programmes and flexible work policies. Look for any unconscious bias hidden in them. For example, do job descriptions or hiring profiles demonstrate age-neutral preferences? Equally, broaden the debate. Involve managers, train them and invite ideas on how your organization can attract and retain older employees. Finally, experiment. Pilot a few programmes involving scale back, job sharing or flexible working. It takes a few years for managers and employees to build large-scale trust in alternative work arrangements and the more successful examples you have today, the more options you will have tomorrow.

> Note: the talent economics toolkit at the end of this book includes a select list of data sources and research publications for those looking to deepen their understanding of changing dependency ratios and ageing populations.

Gender economics

The case for more women leaders

Companies have been saying they need to increase female representation in senior roles for decades, yet the numbers reveal very few are serious. More recently with the popular press and legislature adding their voice to the debate, the call for more women leaders has morphed from a backroom conversation into a very public crescendo. At the bottom of the employment pyramid today we actually find more and more women entering the workforce with each passing decade. Today, 1.2 billion economically active women make up 40 per cent of the 3 billion strong global workforce, but women occupy less than 10 per cent of senior leadership positions across the world's 2,000 largest corporations. This is a grim reality we mustn't avoid.

The slim silver lining, if I can call it that, is the number of women graduating with college degrees is actually on the rise. In 2010, the number of women graduates was at an all-time high and, as a consequence, in many countries the percentage of women in junior management and professional roles is gradually rising too. In the United States, for example, the Department of Labor estimates that over 50 per cent of management and professional positions are held by women (Catalyst Research, 2010). In 1950 when they started tracking women in management, this number was below 14 per cent. This is a reassuring trend, though one that has yet to take root at the top of the management pyramid. Even today, a significant gulf exists between men and women if you tally the gender of CEOs in corporate America. The 2011 list of Fortune 500 companies has just 12 women CEOs, adding up to a dismal gender ratio of 2.4 per cent. One report found that although there are 864 women board members in Fortune 500 boardrooms, men still outnumber them five to one (Soares *et al*, 2010).

The lack of women leaders is a universal issue, and similar stories can be found from all corners of the business world. A study in Australia (EOWA, 2010) found that women were outnumbered nine to one on Australian boards, and a staggering 54 per cent of companies on the ASX 200 had no women board members. This is while women make up 45 per cent of the Australian labour pool and hold over 44.6 per cent of all managerial and professional positions in the economy. Just 3 per cent of the ASX 200 CEOs are female.

In Canada only 12.5 per cent of board seats are held by women (Governance Metrics International, 2010a), in the United Kingdom less than 9 per cent. Emerging markets are much further behind. Brazil and India both have less than 5 per cent each and China 7.2 per cent. On the other hand, the Nordic countries have the highest representation. In Norway one in three board members is a woman, and in Sweden and Finland, one in four.

The lack of women leaders is a significant macro challenge. At a time when complexity is putting a premium on good quality leaders, we find 40 per cent of our workforce without fair opportunity and representation at the top.

The future CEO pipeline

Many companies park this issue somewhere in their HR or diversity team's agenda, which is the totally wrong place for it to take root. The right place is on the CEO's scorecard. Indeed there is a strong case for gender diversity. Improving representation of women in senior roles makes for better decision making, and several studies have shown that companies with more diverse leadership tend to outperform the market. But many companies choose to manoeuvre around this issue by promoting women into non-core or token roles in their executive teams. Hence we find many more women heading staff functions such as HR, operations and business management, than line functions such as general management, marketing and sales. The fact that women CEOs are so few and far between is evidence of this trend. I feel this exacerbates the problem, and reinforces gender biased imagery for certain roles. A senior woman CEO I interviewed a few years ago mentioned the need to be 'more masculine than the men' to be taken seriously. This, more than the numbers, is the core issue we have today. Just having women in the senior team isn't enough. The roles they perform matter too. What we need is a virtuous cycle of women role models who inspire other women to aspire to the top job, and a leadership environment that is gender neutral. This is the CEO's responsibility, and companies that have been successful at fostering an internal pool of women leaders have invariably had a champion right at the top.

A goal can make all the difference

In addition, the organization also needs a gender representation goal woven into business results. Procter & Gamble, for example, has publicly announced an ambition to have half its leadership as women. It already has five women on its 12-member board. This makes business sense for a company with a customer base that is 70 per cent female.

I feel increasing the numbers of women leaders is the single most promising leadership pipeline opportunity for a company operating globally today. It not only helps attract and retain a more diverse pool of talent (remember women outnumber men on college campuses across the world today), it is also increasingly being viewed as part of the overall leadership quality prognosis.

At a country or regional level too this makes macroeconomic sense. Europe is a prime example. We have already seen the talent challenge facing the EU with an ageing population, and low replacement birth rates. By increasing female participation rates at all levels of the workforce, EU countries can alleviate some of this pressure. According to McKinsey & Company, by current estimates Europe will face a shortfall of 24 million workers by 2040. If, however, it manages to raise the rate of employment for women to the same level as men, this shortfall decreases to 3 million workers (McKinsey & Company, 2007).

Generational shifts

My generation Y isn't your generation Y!

Between 2010 and 2020 we will welcome the world's most connected and challenging generation into the workforce. Currently in secondary school and junior college, many call this group generation Z. Apart from being more similar globally than any preceding generation, what makes this group unique is that they were born into a digital world with no boundaries. For this is the internet generation.

Generational studies aren't new. Trait differences between age groups were first highlighted in the late 1980s by two historians, William Strauss and Neil Howe, whose book *Generations* profiled changes to Anglo-American society over five centuries. In what has since come to be known as Strauss and Howe's 'generational theory', they found that, more than anything else, generations were shaped by a common set of experiences during adolescence and young adulthood. This set of common formative experiences shape collective memory and beliefs within a generational cohort, and eventually helps the group form a collective persona, one that is distinct from the preceding generation or the one that follows.

A recent convergence

Generations that grew up during the 20th century had strong nationalistic flavours, as experiences were in most instances local or domestic in nature (the two world wars being the notable exception). More recently, through the impact of television and the internet, early adolescents are increasingly experiencing the world seamlessly and in real time, making them more closely aligned and aware than ever before.

Generational differences form an important part of macro talent behaviour, because generations are motivated differently. They have different expectations from work and thus must be managed differently.

The US interpretation

The bulk of generational research today has roots in North America and Western Europe, two regions with similar open-market economic beliefs, and similar experiences arising out of the world wars and the subsequent Cold War. As a consequence, we find the four US definitions (traditionalist, baby boomers, generation X, generation Y), being used more commonly today.

According to conventional definitions, the traditionalists, born between 1922 and 1945, are also referred to as 'the silent generation'. Strong, disciplined and stable, they lived through the Great Depression, fought the Second World War and then rebuilt the post-war economies. Although most have retired, we still encounter traditionalists in politics, corporate boardrooms and senior policy advisory roles today.

They were followed by the boomers. Named after the baby boom that followed the Second World War, this group rode the successes of booming economic conditions on both sides of the Atlantic – an experience that made them the most economically prosperous generation in history. Born between 1946 and 1964, members of this generation control both government and industry in the Western world today. As the median age of this generation is now in the mid-fifties, they have started retiring in large numbers upon reaching their country's mandatory retirement age.

Next came generation X, aptly named as they were born at the end of the boom economy years, into a more uncertain future. It was a time also marked by a precipitous decline in birth rates as the baby boom ended. Also referred to as the MTV generation, those born between 1965 and 1980 experienced their parents' divorce rates soar, saw increased corporate layoffs affect their elders and they witnessed the Berlin wall fall during early adulthood. As a result, this generation is often characterized as flexible and self-serving, with a deep distrust of authority.

Finally generation Y, born between 1981 and 2000, grew up with a much broader world view, via their early exposure to the internet in the 1990s. They are more discerning about personal ambition, extremely comfortable with diversity and much less hierarchical.

The four US generations are a starting point for understanding generational theory, but by extrapolating this classification globally we invariably commit a grave mistake. Unfortunately, today we frequently encounter both researchers and managers who treat boomer or generation X as a global marker for people in a particular age group. This is wrong, as generational differences are not defined by age or time, but by 'watershed' events during adolescence and early adulthood. It is a fallacy to think that a 49-year-old boomer born and raised in Washington DC thinks and acts like a 49-year-old Moscovite who grew up in communist USSR. As their formative experiences will have been so different, it stands to reason that their traits and motivations will be different too.

Generational tipping points

To study and exemplify how generations are formed within a country or region, we must look for weighty socioeconomic events in history. Specifically, we must look for events big enough to constitute a 'generational marker' for the youth of the time. In simpler terms, a generational marker is a phase or occurrence that causes a country's socioeconomic or political climate to shift.

We began Chapter 1 by discussing the four largest economies of this decade – The United States, China, Japan and India. Each has distinct generational markers and hence different generational cohorts. Generational experiences can be so powerfully unique that even neighbouring countries can be radically dissimilar. China and India share a 3,500-mile-long border, and China has but a narrow sea separating it from Japan, yet all three neighbours have distinctly different generations.

China

The Chinese workforce has had four distinct generational transition points over the last 50 years.

The 1970s and 1980s generation (born in the 1950s and 1960s)

For the current Chinese workforce, the first major generational marker was the Great Cultural Revolution, which lasted 10 years, between 1966 and Chairman Mao's death in 1976. Adolescents and young adults who grew up in this period were deeply affected by the emphasis on totalitarian socialist doctrine, thereby creating a generation of staunch socialists who depended on state patronage, education and employment. The growth of state-owned enterprises and the strict control on agricultural land and housing meant this generation of workers lived deep within the shadow of the state.

The Tiananmen and Reform Generation (born in the 1970s)

From a generational perspective, the next big tipping point was the Tiananmen square protests in 1989, which eventually led to significant reforms led by Deng Xiaoping and Jiang Zemin, the architects of China's socialist market economy. Both were reformers who wanted to adapt Marxism to the times. Young adults who grew up between 1989 and the mid-1990s experienced a period of intense economic reform, modernization and early entrepreneurship in China. Many of them built the manufacturing and export explosion that made the Chinese economy achieve blistering growth between 1991 and 1996. This generation of 45–50 year olds makes up a significant slice of the most affluent entrepreneurs in China today, primarily because they grew up exposed to the earliest version of the Chinese market economy. They are hard working, ambitious and deeply loyal to the Chinese way.

The one-child generation (born in the 1980s)

In 1998 China started an intense phase of educational reform, which saw the number of graduates increase exponentially. Students who grew up in the 1980s were also the first to be taught English as a mainstream subject. More significantly, this period marked the early adulthood of the first urban children born under the 'one-child policy'. As a result, the 2000–10 decade has been one of greater educational achievement, and has resulted in a young workforce with high aspirations. This group tends to focus on rapid career advancement, expecting changes and promotions every other year. They are considerably less loyal too, a factor magnified by a red-hot Chinese economy where jobs are aplenty.

The post-Olympics generation (born 1990–2000)

I believe the Beijing Olympics will in time prove to be another tipping point, giving rise to a generation that truly believes in China's potential as a global superpower. This generation may grow up with global leadership ambitions well beyond Chinese shores, and a desire to see Chinese brands dominate overseas markets.

India

The Indian transformation has been slower than China's and, as a result, the generation tipping points are further apart. There are three broad phases that define the generations in India's workforce today.

The pre-liberalization generation (born 1945–1965)

The assassination of Indian Prime Minster Indira Gandhi in October 1984 was a tipping point like none other. Mrs Gandhi in many ways represented the old socialist guard that had ruled India since independence. Her time in office was characterized by high taxation, a bulging bureaucracy and strict licence control. The Indian economy, at the time a curious mix of inefficient state-owned enterprise and highly entrepreneurial family businesses, was largely closed to the rest of the world. For large private players making a profit was easy as competition was limited and mostly local. The generation that matured in the late 1970s and 1980s were highly loyal, believed in strict hierarchy and hence were firm sponsors of linear careers and tenure-based privileges.

The post-liberalization generation (born 1965–1985)

Indira Gandhi was succeeded by her elder son, Rajiv Gandhi. A youthful 40-year-old, Rajiv had a Western education, was a certified commercial airline pilot, and dreamt of a progressive and economically vibrant India. He built profitable joint ventures with foreign firms, engaged the United States for the first time as an ally and fired up the economic aspirations of India's youth. By 1991 India had begun progressively opening up its economy, and selling off unprofitable government enterprises. Its sizable talent pool welcomed increasing opportunities to work in multinational companies. And almost all aspects of Indian industry – quality, price competitiveness and consumer choice – improved. At the time, many believed India's private sector, which had enjoyed years of low competition, would collapse in the face of global products and services, but this didn't happen. In fact it was the emergence of this generation of managers that redefined India's entrepreneurial potential. This generational cohort has high academic aspirations, deep personal ambition and a willingness to work hard. They were also not afraid to question the status quo or compete globally. It isn't surprising that India has one of the largest contingents of CEOs in the S&P 500 and many come from this generation, as reported in an article entitled 'India's Leading Export CEOs' written by Carla Power and published in *Time Magazine* on 1 August 2011.

The millennial Indians (born 1985–2000)

Since 2000 India has increasingly seen itself as a services giant and the back office of the world. While it largely escaped the dot com bubble, Indian talent has been at the centre of the current century's online business, software and services revolution. India trade body Nasscom estimates India has a market share of 55 per cent of the global outsourced services market, a sector that already contributes more than 6 per cent of the country's GDP (reported in an article published in the *International Business Times* on 3 February 2011 entitled 'India's share in global outsourcing market rises to 55 pct in 2010, says Nasscom'). Those in the generation driving these numbers have high personal and social aspirations, are economically independent from an early age and crave a more balanced lifestyle than their predecessors enjoyed.

Japan

The Dankai (born 1940–1950) and Shirake Sedai (born 1950–1960)

Clubbed together as they share many similar traits, the oldest segments of the Japanese workforce come from the Dankai generation. Born during the Second World War, this group grew up after the allied occupation ended in 1952. The Dankai were the corporate warriors who rebuilt Japan into an economic superpower. Young adults of this era were deeply collective in orientation, and followed well-defined social patterns of life. Work defined life and most Dankai were fiercely dedicated to the organizations they worked for – to the extent that that it was not uncommon to hear of extreme outcomes like 'Karoshi' (death due to overwork), during their prime. Many Dankai women, on the other hand, chose to stay home and dedicated their entire lives to the family, with children at centre of their attention. Eventually, the Dankai's strong work ethic, loyalty to employers and strict social hierarchy left such an omnipotent legacy that its influence lingered well into the following generation, a group often referred to as the Dankai Junior.

In the 1970s and 1980s, the Shirake Sedai or the 'indifferent generation' followed the Dankai into a booming Japanese economy. Seeing affluence and economic success at an early age they were fierce defenders of the Japanese way. As a result, the Shirake Sedai is often seen as a transitional generation that forms a passive bridge between the conservative older generations and the technology savvy future ones.

The Shinjinrui generation (born 1960–1975)

This generation saw the tail end of Japan's economic miracle, a time defined by a boom in Japanese media and computing. As a result, this group revelled in personal gadgetry and consumption of both new media and electronics, eagerly snapping up every new invention that reached the market. Their fascination with animated media and alternate reality also fuelled the anime craze that swept Japan in the 1990s, and still persists today.

The post-bubble (born 1975–1990) and Yutori (born 1990–2000)

Probably the hardest done by, those in this cohort were born into a rich country with immense personal wealth and a host of material comforts, yet were confronted by an economy that had started stagnating after years of blistering growth. In the early 1990s Japan's asset bubble burst, and both land and stock prices collapsed. This had a devastating effect on Japan's economic model and was an increasingly confusing time for the generation graduating from schools and colleges. Many companies abolished their lifetime employment systems and increased reliance on contract employees and personnel employment agencies instead of hiring full-time employees. Japan remains one of the most affluent places on earth, and had enjoyed such a strong legacy of economic success that few in this generation expected economic decline to last as long as it has. More recently, things have started to improve and with mass retirement of the Dankai, new jobs and opportunities have started to appear for younger generations.

An imperative for global managers

As we can see, seismic socioeconomic events cause generations to tip. And with local realities being so different, there is no such thing as a South African baby boomer or a Chinese generation Y. What's more, the world's four largest economies have four entirely independent sets of generational markers. From an organizational perspective, understanding generation markers for different countries can provide a fascinating management insight into cultural and motivational differences at the workplace. It has macro talent economic implications because it can also help us predict differences in behaviour, expectations and management style across key talent markets. As a leader, I realized this the hard way, in a very personal experience outlined below.

CASE STUDY

In 2007, the constituent mix of my direct team looked like this:

- two from Singapore;

- one from England;

- one Australian;

- two Indians;

- one Hong Kong Chinese;

- one Japanese;

- one Filipino.

Those in this team came from different age groups, were based across the region, and each headed an independent geography or product. As a leader, it was fascinating to watch each country demonstrate distinct cultural and generational preferences in the decisions it made, a fact that sometimes did lead to the odd misunderstandings or conflict.

It was clear fairly early on that if we wanted to be a benchmark team – which hired, retained and grew the best talent – we would need to understand and appreciate our differences better. So we began investing a portion of each face-to-face meeting towards deciphering our individual cultural and generational codes. Not only was this a fun activity for the group, it increased our appreciation of interpersonal context, and each other's opinion.

In a globally connected world, this is a reality we will increasingly have to get used to. As an example, three out of seven newly minted engineers and management graduates today are either Indian or Chinese. For managers across the world, understanding generational markers in both these countries can be an invaluable global management insight.

Future talent – through the crystal ball

High school proficiency

I believe the strongest predictor of the long-term prospects for an economy is the quality of its formative education system. If you spend a few minutes thinking about it, the logic in this argument emerges quite naturally. As we have already seen above, natural wealth can't be the strongest predictor of economic success. If so, the average incomes in Saudi Arabia, Libya, Brazil and Nigeria would not trail resource-poor countries such as Switzerland, Singapore or Taiwan. Success can't be guaranteed purely by the quality of governance and institutions, for the best governed and least corrupt countries are actually barely able to grow today. Finally, it can't just be the quantum of talent available – some of the world's largest populations, for example Indonesia (the fourth largest), Pakistan (sixth largest) and Nigeria (seventh largest) have struggled to live up to their demographic potential, in spite of having workforces filled with youthful aspiration.

The quality of formative education, on the other hand, is a very powerful enabler, for it unlocks potential. It gives millions of young aspirations the opportunity for fulfilment.

Many years ago, I bought my two-year-old son a box of pencils on the way home from work. His eyes lit up, and we sat down together to draw what must have seemed to him like magical lines on two large sheets stolen from the dot matrix printer in my study. But when we opened the box of pencils, none of them were sharpened. It took me a precious 10 minutes to rummage and painfully discovered we didn't have a pencil sharpener at home. I finally got one from the neighbours and we got down to business, yet this experience taught me a small lesson that has proven invaluable – **a talented and plentiful workforce can amount to a box of blunt pencils unless it has access to the basic education needed to sharpen skills and intellect**.

For business leaders and talent managers, basic educational proficiency is a key insight into macro talent economics. Countries with stronger educational performance tend to have smarter workers and a stronger learning ethic, which is critical in a fast-paced world. They are also able grow and leverage technology better. In fact, the potential pipeline of scientists, mathematicians and researchers can be clearly seen through the mathematics and science scores of pre-university students. And you don't even need a crystal ball to do so.

The OECD (Organization for Economic Co-operation and Development) is a Paris-based association of 34 member countries. Mainly representing the free market economies in the developed world, the OECD is a powerful association with wide ranging influence on international economic policy.

In 1997, the OECD set up an office to design and administer a measure of literacy standards across its member countries. The first Programme for International Student Assessment (PISA) test was administered to more than 250,000 students across 30 countries in 2000. Three more tests have been conducted since then, in 2003, 2006 and 2009. Over these four assessments, the PISA has grown in stature as the gold standard for educational literacy testing, with well-designed examinations administered globally by independent assessors under high-quality supervision. So much so, that several non-OECD countries now volunteer to have their students tested and benchmarked. The test is administered to 15-year-old students on three dimensions: reading, mathematics and science. In the 2009 edition, a record number of over half a million students in 67 countries sat for the two-hour long PISA examination.

Sputnik revisited

Finland has traditionally outperformed other OECD economies on the PISA examinations, and Canada, New Zealand, South Korea and Japan also enjoy consistently strong performances on these tests. The 2009 test, however, threw up a major surprise. For the first time ever schools from mainland China participated, with students from the Shanghai school district taking the PISA examination. The results are shown in Table 4.6.

China topping all three tests was a wake-up call for educators in many developed countries. An article by Chester Finn published in the *Wall Street Journal* on 8 December 2010 was entitled 'A Sputnik Moment for US Education', in famous reference to the emotions felt across the United States when the USSR became the first nation to put a man-made object in space late in 1957.

Education standards are an emotional subject and hence any attempt to benchmark them is invariably prone to criticism. This is why the PISA administrators engineer a meticulous examination,

TABLE 4.6 Programme for International Student Assessment (2009)

Rank	Reading	score	Mathematics	score	Science	score
-	PISA Average	493	PISA Average	496	PISA Average	501
1	China	556	China	600	China	575
2	Korea	539	Singapore	562	Finland	554
3	Finland	536	Hong Kong	555	Hong Kong	549
4	Hong Kong	533	Korea	546	Singapore	542
5	Singapore	526	Chinese Taipei	543	Japan	539
6	Canada	524	Finland	541	Korea	538
7	New Zealand	521	Liechtenstein	536	New Zealand	532
8	Japan	520	Switzerland	534	Canada	529
9	Australia	515	Japan	529	Estonia	528
10	Netherlands	508	Canada	527	Australia	527
11	Belgium	506	Netherlands	526	Netherlands	522
12	Norway	503	China: Macao	525	Chinese Taipei	520
13	Estonia	501	New Zealand	519	Liechtenstein	520
14	Switzerland	501	Belgium	515	Germany	520
15	Iceland	500	Australia	514	Switzerland	517
16	Poland	500	Germany	513	United Kingdom	514
17	United States	500	Estonia	512	Slovenia	512
18	Liechtenstein	499	Iceland	507	China: Macao	511
19	Germany	497	Denmark	503	Poland	508
20	Sweden	497	Slovenia	501	Ireland	508
21	France	496	Norway	498	Belgium	507
22	Ireland	496	France	497	Hungary	503
23	Chinese Taipei	495	Slovak Republic	497	United States	502
24	Denmark	495	Austria	496	Norway	500
25	Hungary	494	Poland	495	Czech Republic	500
26	United Kingdom	494	Sweden	494	Denmark	499
27	Portugal	489	Czech Republic	493	France	498
28	China: Macao	487	United Kingdom	492	Iceland	496
29	Italy	486	Hungary	490	Sweden	495
30	Latvia	484	Luxembourg	489	Austria	494
31	Greece	483	United States	487	Latvia	494
32	Slovenia	483	Ireland	487	Portugal	493
33	Spain	481	Portugal	487	Lithuania	491

TABLE 4.6 *Continued*

Rank	Reading	score	Mathematics	score	Science	score
34	Czech Republic	478	Italy	483	Slovak Republic	490
35	Slovak Republic	477	Spain	483	Italy	489
36	Croatia	476	Latvia	482	Spain	488
37	Israel	474	Lithuania	477	Croatia	486
38	Luxembourg	472	Russian Fed.	468	Luxembourg	484
39	Austria	470	Greece	466	Russian Fed.	478
40	Lithuania	468	Croatia	460	Greece	470
41	Turkey	464	Dubai (UAE)	453	Dubai (UAE)	466
42	Dubai (UAE)	459	Israel	447	Israel	455
43	Russian Fed.	459	Turkey	445	Turkey	454
44	Chile	449	Serbia	442	Chile	447
45	Serbia	442	Azerbaijan	431	Serbia	443
46	Bulgaria	429	Bulgaria	428	Bulgaria	439
47	Uruguay	426	Uruguay	427	Romania	428
48	Mexico	425	Romania	427	Uruguay	427
49	Romania	424	Chile	421	Thailand	425
50	Thailand	421	Mexico	419	Mexico	416
51	Trinidad &Tobago	416	Thailand	419	Jordan	415
52	Colombia	413	Trinidad &Tobago	414	Trinidad &Tobago	410
53	Brazil	412	Kazakhstan	405	Brazil	405
54	Montenegro	408	Montenegro	403	Colombia	402
55	Jordan	405	Argentina	388	Montenegro	401
56	Tunisia	404	Jordan	387	Argentina	401
57	Indonesia	402	Brazil	386	Tunisia	401
58	Argentina	398	Colombia	381	Kazakhstan	400
59	Kazakhstan	390	Albania	377	Albania	391
60	Albania	385	Tunisia	371	Indonesia	383
61	Qatar	372	Indonesia	371	Qatar	379
62	Panama	371	Qatar	368	Panama	376
63	Peru	370	Peru	365	Azerbaijan	373
64	Azerbaijan	362	Panama	360	Peru	369
65	Kyrgyzstan	314	Kyrgyzstan	331	Kyrgyzstan	330

SOURCE: OECD, PISA 2009 (www.oecd.org/dataoecd/54/12/46643496.pdf).

with exacting standards. For example, educators across the world contribute to the test questions, and the test itself is offered in 50 languages globally to ensure that students have an equal opportunity to compete. It is also independently administered, supervised and scored, and each edition's technical provisions are freely shared and welcome to scrutiny.

Benchmarking students puts the quality of education under scrutiny. Low scores don't signify lower intelligence levels among students. In fact, various other factors impact PISA performance, for example the socioeconomic backgrounds students come from, class sizes, the private or public nature of schools in the sample, and whether the school is in an urban or rural area. All these factors have an impact on performance in subtle yet material ways. Even countries with the highest scores have schools that perform below the PISA average. In totality though, this is as good a report card as any on the importance education is given within the political and administration frame-works across countries. The quality of curriculum, quality of teaching, and student–teacher relationships all have a direct correlation to PISA performance. In spite of education reform being a long and arduous process, educators and politicians who take this test seriously can do wonders for educational proficiency among future generations. Professor Eric A Hanushek from the Hoover Institution at Stanford University and Professor Ludger Woessmann from the University of Munich, who have studied how an increase in PISA scores correlates strongly with actual economic progress, say:

'Changing schools and educational institutions is, of course, a difficult task. Moreover, countries that have attempted reforms of schools have often found that the results in terms of student achievement are relatively modest. At the same time, the results from countries achieving high and equitable learning outcomes in PISA – like Finland in Europe, Canada in North America or Japan and Korea in East Asia – or from those that have seen rapid improvements in the quality of schooling (like Poland) underline that doing better is possible' (OECD, 2010).

A case of political will

In reality, there are 13 countries that managed to improve reading levels among their students between PISA 2000 and 2009 examina-tions. These are Chile, Indonesia, Peru, Albania, Portugal, Poland, Israel,

Liechtenstein, Brazil, Latvia, Hungary, Germany and Korea. Of these 13 countries, the first 12 did this by primarily improving the educational performance of their lowest performers (the bottom 10 per cent of students). Korea on the other hand, which had a very high standard to begin with, worked on making its top performers even better.

Your future managers, scientists and engineers

The reason business leaders need to have an interest in the academic performance of 15-year-olds across the world is quite clear. Early proficiency has a direct impact on career aspirations, access to higher education and entrepreneurial ability. And, in turn, all these factors affect our supply of critical entry-level talent. Indirectly, early proficiency also sets the stage for managerial competence, learning culture and career velocity. In countries where early proficiency lags, companies will need to invest more in improving the skills of new junior employees upfront when they join. Similarly, there could be a greater need for mid-career development higher up the ranks.

What is most important though is that broad macro trends are visible in secondary education itself. The better the quality of educational competence in secondary school, the richer the pipeline of talent entering the workforce a few short years later. Better-quality education eventually translates into more managers, professionals, scientists, engineers and entrepreneurs. This correlates very well with GDP performance too, as a high-quality talent pool is a critical ingredient for both new businesses to take root and older businesses to flourish and grow.

Quality of young talent is one dimension; the other is the quantity of this talent coming through the educational system with skills relevant to business, in particular the number of students continuing to study beyond higher secondary levels. Across the world, the UN and educational policy makers closely track changes to a country's gross enrolment ratio (GER) at each stage of the education process. Simply put, the GER is a statistical index that demonstrates the percentage of students actually enrolled in the schooling system, when compared to the overall population eligible for education. For example, the GER for a secondary school system is the number of

12–17-year-olds enrolled in school compared to the total number of 12–17-year-olds in the country.

On to further education

As talent economists particularly interested in understanding the flow of business relevant education in an economy, a number that should interest us is the tertiary enrolment ratio (TER) for a country. This measures the number of students choosing to continue education beyond senior secondary school. By comparing changes to enrolment numbers over time, it is fairly easy to predict increases or decreases in the pipeline of skilled talent available to business.

At a macro level, the world's TER hovers around 27 per cent (World Bank, 2012). In most high-income countries, more than 60 per cent of secondary school graduates enrol in further education. The corresponding number in the world's lowest income countries is well below 10 per cent. Hidden between these two extremes are some fascinating insights. For example, trends tell us that over the last 10 years alone China has raised tertiary enrolments by over 200 per cent. While its overall enrolment is still relatively low at 24 per cent, consider that in 1980 this number was below 2 per cent. Poland, Malaysia, Mongolia, Cuba, Venezuela and Ukraine have also seen appreciable increases in tertiary education numbers. This bodes well from a macro talent supply perspective.

Brazil and India, on the other hand, have been relative under-performers. The gross enrolment in India as an example is well below 15 per cent. For a country with a long and rich educational heritage, this number has barely crept up over the last 20 years.

A business opportunity

While China's story has been driven by aggressive educational reforms and government-backed investments in higher education, in India it is the government that has proved a stumbling block. But like so much of India's growth story, where the government misses the boat the Indian private sector always sniffs out a business opportunity. One such example is the ambitious vocational training company IndiaCan.

CASE STUDY   IndiaCan

A young business, backed by aggressive private equity and some of the world's largest educational providers, IndiaCan has rocketed up the charts as a serious career enabler for thousands of Indian youth. The CEO, Sharad Talwar, spells out the opportunity for his company. 'At a gross enrolment ratio of less than 15 per cent, there is serious risk to India sustaining its blistering economic growth in the long run. This number should be brought close to 30 or 40 per cent.' Sharad clearly sees the opportunity and has helped build a company focused on enrolling unemployed 18–30-year-olds into its highly practical specialist programmes. 'It doesn't matter if they are school or college drop outs,' Talwar says, 'without skills they have no options, no access to jobs. That is where we come in.'

IndiaCan runs basic programmes in spoken English and basic computing, followed by specialist programmes in sales, retail, healthcare, journalism, accounting and IT; all backed by international certifications. Business isn't just good – it's booming. There is copious demand for IndiaCan's students within India's burgeoning services sector and, as a result, after only a few years this educational factory today churns out skilled employees by the thousands. When I spoke with Talwar, he was in the midst of lobbying banks to include vocational training courses within the ambit of student loans – a move that could take the private mass-education industry to a whole new level.

Basic proficiency is a very powerful macro indicator for a country's talent pipeline. Considering both the qualitative and quantitative aspects of education, business can build a much more focused talent acquisition and development strategy. **In business today, it is critical that a five-year business plan is built on an underlying five-year talent viewpoint.**

Note: The talent economics toolkit at the end of this book includes a select list of data sources and research publications for those looking to deepen their understanding of high school proficiency and gross enrolment trends.

Management proficiency

Basic proficiency gives us clues about a society's innate orientation to learning. Countries with consistently high scores achieve them by placing a premium on learning and performance. Eventually this raises a workforce's overall learning agility. However, proficiency in high school is only the first educational step towards future jobs or entrepreneurship. The second step is equally critical and deals with the quality and applicability of tertiary education to business. In simple terms, the question is: Are the skills of our future engineers, managers and professionals closely aligned to business realities outside the classroom? Unlike basic proficiency, which can be measured via objective scores, grades have limited meaning in the business world. What matters more is that education meets the needs of the business community and can be built upon when a student joins his or her first job.

Analysing the quality of undergraduate and graduate education is an important input when deciding where to hire fresh talent, and how to groom employees in the early years on the job. This is because approaches and standards of management education are so different at a global level that it is difficult to use the same yardstick for all graduates. And there is profound insight in studying the numbers. Let's take management education in India and China as an example.

A world apart

By 2020, both India and China will have enhanced their position as important growth engines in the global economy. High growth also makes both countries insatiably hungry for fresh management talent today. Unfortunately, that's where the similarity stops. China and India differ materially, both on the number of graduates they produce and the quality of education provided. India has close to 2,000 postgraduate management institutions accredited by the AICTE (India's technical training council), which collectively enrols around 180,000 students each year. This number is massive. By comparison, the United States graduates approximately 156,000 MBAs each year (NumberOf.net, 2010). For China on the other hand, management education is a relatively new concept. Not many people realize that

China had just nine MBA programmes in 1991, when educational reforms started. This number has grown with the Chinese government's focus and investment in management education, yet sprouting off such small roots means that today China has just 236 business schools – in contrast to India's 2,000 – a number woefully inadequate for an economy of its size. A recent article that commented on China's management education puts the current number of management graduates at around 20,000 per year (Scrimenti, 2010). Compare this with the views of John Quelch, Vice President of the highly rated China Europe International Business School (CEIBS) in Shanghai. An updated account of an interview with Quelch, written by Gao Changxin and entitled 'VP Calls for More MBA Programs', was published in *China Daily* on 11 April 2011. In the interview Quelch estimated the Chinese economy could absorb 600,000 management graduates a year. That's the war for talent in China right there.

As a talent economist, I count the lack of a robust management pipeline as China's most significant talent risk. And that's not just because of the low numbers, or the years it will take to catch up with the other economic superpowers. It's costing China more and more of its precious young talent in the short run too. Driven by the shortage of opportunities for management education at home, more and more of China's best scholars are looking overseas. In 2010, more than 80,000 Chinese students applied to US MBA programmes alone, as reported in an article entitled 'China Send More Students to US Business Schools Than India This Year' published in the *International Business Times* on 30 September 2010. Apart from sheer size, what is significant is that China's talent drain has steadily accelerated each year over the past decade – at a time when the Chinese economy needed its best and brightest the most.

At a macro level, the pipeline of future managers is a direct outcome of tertiary education activity in a market system. Great education not only helps improve capability of youth within the country but is also a magnet of the best talent from overseas. Over the last 40 years or more, countries such the United States, the United Kingdom, Australia and Singapore, among others, have benefited immensely via their overseas student populations choosing to stay on and join the local economy after graduation.

Beyond the degree – quality matters more

The quantum of graduates is a starting point of macro analysis, but going beyond quantity how do we assess the quality of management education across the world? Global MBA school rankings are one option. And while they never fail to stir up debate on criteria selection and fair representation, these lists are powerful influencers for both students and recruiters alike. As a strategist I would recommend only a high-level view of these rankings. By covering just the top 100 or 200 schools globally, and with relatively few schools outside of the United States and Europe on the list, they have limited utility from a macro talent perspective. I do watch them for subtler cues though: Where is the quality of management education on the rise? Where is it on the decline? Which schools represent a more international mix of students and faculty? Who do the recruiters prefer?

At a local level, to assess the efficacy of management education, the three operative questions I like to answer are:

1 Are our new graduate hires acutely aware of business climate and conditions?

2 Can they assume a practical view and apply the knowledge and skills they learnt in school?

3 How much investment is required in the early years to round off their ability and make them productive?

Answering these questions help business managers cultivate an informed opinion on talent proficiency across key hiring markets. At a global level, one of the best references to help us compare management proficiency comes from the World Competitiveness Centre, started in 1989 by Professor Stéphane Garelli at European business school IMD. The centre publishes an annual World Competitiveness Report that uses over 300 criteria to compare the conditions for business in 59 countries. An integral part of the research is an executive opinion survey, which in 2011 was answered by almost 5,000 executives across the world.

In part, this survey deals with graduate proficiency and in specific terms the quality of management education across the world. The question of whether 'management education meets the needs of the business community' produced surprising responses. The traditional

FIGURE 4.6 Executive opinion on whether 'management education meets the needs of the business community' (2010 and 2011 scores compared)

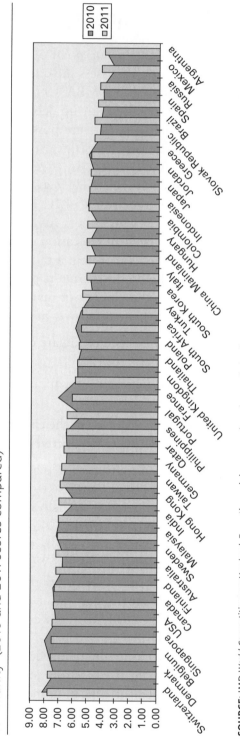

SOURCE: IMD *World Competitiveness Yearbook* Executive opinion survey based on an index from 0 to 10 . IMD World Competitiveness online, 1995–2011 (updated May 2011), see also www.imd.org/research/publications/wcy/wcy_book.cfm

leaders in management education such as the United States or the United Kingdom were not at the top of the list. The top three countries were Switzerland, Denmark and Belgium. The United States comes in fifth, behind Singapore, and the United Kingdom somewhere in the middle of the pack. Perceptions matter and I would submit that executives' opinion on graduate quality is the real 'proof of the pudding' for management education. Figure 4.6 represents how executives scored across a number of important world economies.

Note: The talent economics toolkit at the end of this book includes a select list of data sources and research publications for those looking to deepen their understanding of tertiary education trends and management proficiency.

Corporate governance and sustainability

The last macro variable is probably the most important to those in leadership positions, given the plethora of corporate scandals we have witnessed in recent history. The truth, as the 2009 financial crisis showed us, is that it is getting more and more difficult to agree on a universally accepted standard of regulation and governance across the world. Documented instances of fraud, cases of irresponsible management, jailed executives and regulatory fines paid are only the tip of this iceberg. Yes, we learn important lessons from them, but for every known instance, one can only speculate how many grey decisions and cut corners go unreported. In an era where every country is regulated differently, one of the fallouts of greater globalization is an increase in governance grey areas, ethical dilemmas and regulatory loopholes, be it safety standards or hazardous waste disposal in a low-cost manufacturing location, or a pharmaceutical company continuing to sell banned drugs in low-regulation markets. What is illegal in one country may be considered a commonly accepted business practice in another.

Many senior managers I have spoken with are deeply worried about the increasing complexity they face in governing a global business. They know the deal – the buck stops with them, even for questionable decisions made by local management in a far-flung outpost. **While mistakes may be local, in today's connected world embarrassment is global.**

There is broad-based agreement that organizations need to pay more importance to internal governance. Given vast differences in standards, and an increasingly mobile global workforce, the question isn't **if** blow-ups will happen, it's **when.**

Before drafting strategy, there are two areas I suggest for global analysis. The first is the emphasis in a market system on good governance. The second is the focus on corporate social responsibility (CSR) and sustainable business practices. Looking at both together we can generate a simple risk profile for global business to act upon.

The spotlight on corporate governance

Local managers operate under a set of complex influences. The questions we must answer for every country we manage are:

- What are the norms of business in the country in question?
- What is the regulatory framework?
- How strong are the behavioural benchmarks, exemplified through the prominent economic, social and political role models in the country?
- How strong is leadership accountability?
- How evolved is the framework of laws covering white-collar crime?

Collectively, these questions help profile the circumstances for responsible management in a country. In addition, at a global level, we also need data sources that can help compare one environment to another. There are two sources that help us.

The Worldwide Governance Indicators

The World Bank, sponsors of the annual Worldwide Governance Indicators (WGI) study, describes governance as '... the traditions and institutions by which authority in a country is exercised. This includes the process by which governments are selected, monitored and replaced; the capacity of the government to effectively formulate and implement sound policies; and the respect of citizens and the state for the institutions that govern economic and social interactions among them' (World Bank Group, 2011).

The WGI profiles over 200 countries and territories on measures such as voice and accountability, political stability and absence of violence/terrorism, government effectiveness, regulatory quality, rule of law, and control of corruption (Kaufmann, Kraay and Mastruzzi, 2010).

While WGI comments on the quality of institutions, economic freedom, political stability and a host of other factors that facilitate economic activity, it isn't the best metric for corporate governance. In recent years a number of private and country rating services have begun filling this space.

Corporate governance country rankings

Institutional Shareholders Services (ISS) publishes the Corporate Governance Quotient, which has close to 8,000 companies profiled. Rating agencies such as Standard & Poor's also profile companies before they issue in-depth corporate governance reports; Governance Metrics International (GMI) started the trend in 2000 and now publishes governance ratings on over 5,000 companies globally. GMI also releases country rankings for governance.

In the GMI corporate governance country rankings released in September 2010 the United Kingdom, Canada, Ireland, the United States and New Zealand held the top five spots (Governance Metrics International, 2010b). South Africa, with 43 firms profiled, did surprisingly well, being placed ninth globally. South Africa is in great company, with Finland just above it and Sweden just below. Germany was at position 12, Singapore at 17 and India in the middle of the list at 20. The lower quartiles threw up many surprises. While it may not surprise many to see Brazil (30) Russia (31) and China (35) in the lower half, South Korea at 28 and Hong Kong at 26 are surprising. Hong Kong, with a large sample of 72 companies profiled, is especially significant as it regularly tops a number of global polls as one of the easiest countries to do business in. Equally surprising was Japan's position, fourth from the bottom. With a large sample of 392 Japanese companies in the GMI database, this doesn't augur well for Japanese business prospects.

In recent years, several country-based rating initiatives have also emerged. Singapore's Governance and Transparency Index (GTI) is a good case in point.

CASE STUDY   Singapore's GTI

Singapore is a great example of clean governance and helpful settings for business to prosper. In 2000 the *Business Times* and the National University of Singapore's Centre for Governance, Institutions and Organizations set up the GTI. The index studies and ranks Singaporean companies on boardroom accountability, the quality of disclosure and how well a company communicates with its shareholders. In the 2011 list, 687 companies were ranked based on performance (*Business Times*/Centre for Governance, Institutions and Organizations, 2011).

What were the results? On a 100-point scale, 92 per cent of companies didn't make it past 50 (*Singapore Business Review*, 2011).

It is a focus on analysis and disclosure that makes management more accountable at a country level. From our perspective, studying corporate governance trends allows us to prioritize the training of local managers and build a strong culture of accountability in countries where the external environment is weak. And don't expect your compliance department to do this; high-quality governance is part of every manager's pay cheque.

Management and the art of responsible business

As recently as 10 years ago, it was difficult to find the words 'social responsibility' in the competency models used to hire, promote and reward managers. Today, if they don't exist we seriously doubt the organization's commitment to responsible business practice. In the past, sustainability wasn't the job of individual managers; it was something the CSR department did on the sidelines. Managers were there to drive results, and the CSR team conjured up a few projects that looked good in the annual report. Today, however, sustainability is a primary issue facing both countries and organizations alike. The world has changed.

Some countries do better than others on a commitment to sustainable business practice, and have a regulatory framework to back it up. While there is no credible system to rank management competence and commitment to sustainability, several rankings exist that aim to rank both countries and companies globally. These studies are a good starting point to gauge accountability in practice. Countries with stronger regulation, better policies and best practices are ranked higher and there are strong chances local managers would have been trained to take this responsibility seriously.

Two top US universities, Yale and Columbia, produce the Environmental Performance Index (EPI), a very comprehensive global ranking system for countries across the world. The EPI 'ranks 163 countries on 25 performance indicators tracked across ten well-established policy categories covering both environmental public health and ecosystem vitality. These indicators provide a gauge at a national government scale of how close countries are to established environmental policy goals' (Yale University, 2010).

It must be said upfront that ranking countries can be controversial, as many would argue emerging economies are at a technology disadvantage and have more pressing issues, such as poverty, to tackle first. Yet a country's policy approach to the environment and sustainability can be compared to its peers' and more importantly to its own goals. In similar circumstances, countries that start earlier and focus more on sustainability will win in the long term.

Another place to look is a number of ranking lists for companies committed to sustainable business. The presence of more companies from a particular country on such a list is important. They serve as role models to others on the ground and incubate local best practices in socially responsible business. Rankings exist at a country level too, and some basic research can help us analyse who are the benchmark organizations at local levels.

As people strategists, attentiveness to the external environment can inform our development decisions in the company. We may need to invest more in training managers in a country where the external regulatory environment isn't as strong, and hence warrants more internal inquiry and support. As an example, Iceland ranks number 1 on the EPI 2010 list, and Canada number 46.

Note: The talent economics toolkit at the end of this book includes a select list of data sources and research publications for those looking to deepen their understanding of governance and sustainability rankings and trends.

Organizational leaders looking to lay out strategy for 2020 and beyond can use macro talent trends to provide valuable subtext to critical talent decisions. Smart companies realize they need mechanisms and insight to tackle the inherent complexity of global business. Analysing the eight macro variables build critical context, highlight subtle differences and help craft proactive response to changes in market conditions.

Trading the telescope for a magnifying glass

The global workforce is made up of 3 billion individuals, each on a personal journey. **To better understand behaviour in a collective, we must also seek to understand the motive of the individual.** That brings us to micro talent economics.

Micro talent economics
Managing the 21st-century employee

05

'Time and space are modes by which we think and not conditions in which we live.' **ALBERT EINSTEIN**

Macro analysis helps us identify operative trends and predict how a country's employment environment will change over the next 10 or 20 years. When you overlay this macro environment with your own organization's growth or business strategy, it is easy to identify which talent investments are a priority and which are wasteful.

The study of aggregate talent is a strong starting point. It provides a powerful underlay for a variety of talent management decisions. However, from a day-to-day perspective, just the big picture view isn't enough. For one, it can't predict changes in individual behaviour. To do so we must also understand how the circumstances surrounding the individual employee are changing, and equally how the overall relationship between an employee and employer is changing. I call this the study of micro talent economics.

FIGURE 5.1 Both macro and micro perspectives are important

Macro talent economics

Micro talent economics

Micro talent economics helps us find the right talent as well as improve the way we train, motivate and reward our existing talent today. In a rapidly evolving world, it helps us align the organization to its employees.

From open door to open plan

The business of employment has changed quite dramatically since the 1980s. Back then employees looked for stable organizations that could guarantee them a long-term career. Seniority mattered immensely, as did long-term benefits.

Organizations looked different. Most companies back then were complex social arrangements, best exemplified by tall hierarchical structures and linear career paths.

Early in my career I remember reading an HR handbook that listed 30 employment layers sandwiched between board members at the top and the apprentice at the bottom. Employees at each level, as this 100-page manual intricately explained, enjoyed an elaborately differentiated set of perquisites, including where they could eat.

Walking to the cafeteria, I was forced to pass the elaborate dining facilities designated for senior executives, followed by the slightly less opulent middle managers' lunchroom. The company car grew at each level too, and specifications were so tightly controlled that it was easy to find out who was being paid more just by hanging around the car park or by walking past people's offices. Senior managers had a little round table in a corner and vice presidents got a small sofa in addition. If you were a high performer, you could expect mementoes and holidays to be handed out at quarterly recognition events; and the bonus was a flat multiple of salary, paid in good years to all employees. This was clearly a time before open-plan offices, flexible working, middle-management stock awards and now omnipotent variable incentive programmes.

Management was different too. Taller structures meant fewer direct reports, and the 'employee of the month' programme actually did help motivate performance. In fact, in the early 1980s, the best way to gauge employee engagement was through the number of complaints that found their way into the suggestion box.

A foundational shift

The employment transaction has evolved a fair way since then. Starting with the portability of benefits we discussed in Chapter 1, the increase in cash-based reward programmes and escalating re-engineering activity, we have seen the emotional bond between the employee and employer weaken with each passing decade.

On the one hand, companies have become more comfortable about making employees redundant at the first sign of economic turbulence. On the other hand, with historically low economic disincentive for leaving, employees today have an expanded career horizon and look well beyond their current organizations for career opportunities.

The employment equation used to be built on a foundation of two-way loyalty. The world has changed. Today, successful employment relationships can only be sustained on a foundation of two-way honesty.

This isn't a minor shift, or one that can be met by adjusting a few policies. Rather, there is now a legitimate demand for management practices of old to evolve too.

In this chapter we will look forward, seeking to understand what the employee–employer relationship in the future will look like, and how that changes the way we manage our most precious resource today. We will focus on seven progressive management practices. They are not silver bullets, but rather an invitation to think differently. The aim is to outline a framework of ideas that resonate with the 21st-century employee.

The seven indispensable practices for 2020 are:

1 Shift focus from finding the best talent to finding the right talent.
2 Open the door – build unconventional entry points for talent.
3 Poach your talent before the competition does.
4 Create an expansive mindset – champion diversity of thought.
5 Open the window – think outside-in.
6 Help innovation thrive – create organizational flow.
7 Measure and grow cerebral engagement.

Let's explore each one in turn.

1. Focus on finding the right talent

Sell your reality

Talent is more mobile than ever before, which in turn means the revolving door at the office reception is working harder than ever. New people will join you and some will leave, that is the hard truth. Yet to the smart organization, this presents an opportunity. Because every opportunity to hire is an opportunity to press reset – to recalibrate new employee expectations to reality.

To begin with, 'sell your reality' sounds a lot less exciting than 'find the best talent available'. It may also sound paradoxical at first. After all, we are bang in the middle of a global war for talent, so shouldn't our goal be to upgrade – to go after the best resumes in the market with every opportunity? True, if you are only focused on hiring. Evidence and our own experiences tell us that while finding talent is hard, getting talent to stay and be successful is harder.

CASE STUDY

A small private bank, known for its bespoke wealth management solutions, was struggling to retain new employees beyond a year or two. Many candidates from larger banks were keen to join this bank at higher salaries but soon realized that the lack of sophistication in a smaller (and more entrepreneurial) unit meant the jobs were quite different from what they had anticipated. This was leading to disillusionment and the eventual departure of many promising new hires. The exit interviews clearly showed a mismatch between expectations and reality.

In hindsight, the bank's HR team, together with the hiring managers, could have done a much better job at highlighting the 'real' positives of working for the bank – greater flexibility, empowerment and opportunity for entrepreneurship.

And herein lies the issue. The bank had no problem attracting the best talent, but was it attracting the right talent? Was it finding talent that would thrive in the circumstances on offer? Maybe not. In this particular case, there was no coordinated approach, no common language or alignment on how roles were being positioned. Unfortunately, this is a common error that organizations are doomed to make unless they learn to calibrate candidate expectations in a more deliberate, precise and coordinated manner.

Offer a value proposition

Marketing has used the concept of customer value propositions (CVPs) for decades. In its simplest form, a CVP is the sum total of benefits the seller promises customers in exchange for their business. A powerful CVP can help differentiate a product from its competitors and ensure that the right attributes stand out in a crowded marketplace.

It works wonders internally too. Well before a product reaches the shop window, back at the drawing board, a well-defined CVP helps align product development, research and sales efforts. And the CVP gets them all working together to ensure that the right benefits are developed, advertised and eventually delivered.

More recently, and as a direct result of the war for talent, the HR function has started developing and using its own version of the CVP to drive talent sourcing efforts. Called the employee value proposition (EVP), it helps advertise the specific attributes of a company that could prove attractive to potential employees, with a clear aim to promise exactly what can be delivered.

Similar to the CVP, a well-formulated EVP allows an organization to highlight and sell its employment experience in a deliberate, consistent and transparent manner. In a large diversified organization, this is imperative if it wants to avoid the risk of every hiring manager positioning the organization differently to candidates.

There is sound logic in using an EVP at the core of your talent attraction efforts. Here are the most compelling reasons why:

- Every new employee and new employer want to make a great first impression. The first 90 days are critical in ensuring a long-term employment relationship. It is here that a well-formulated EVP can make all the difference. It helps accelerate early resonance, which has a direct correlation on employees' success and intent to stay.

- We want a candidate to hear consistent messages irrespective of the channel they receive it from. Recruitment advertisements, head hunters, HR interviewers and hiring managers all play a role in setting candidates' expectations. A consistent and well-formulated EVP keeps recruitment advertising aligned to a set of central messages. We don't want to oversell the organization to candidates just to get them through the door, only to have the actual experience disappoint them later. In a recent research study (WorldatWork and Towers Watson, 2010) covering 1,100 HR professionals across the world, 34 per cent said their companies had a formal EVP. When this group was asked if their company did a good job at communicating its employment attributes, 74 per cent of respondents said that it did. The results were dramatically different in the companies that didn't have a formal EVP, where less than one in five respondents answered positively.

- Over time, a clear value proposition helps create a strong employment brand that becomes more widely known and recognized. Today, due to well-managed advertising and publicity efforts, most candidates know that Google encourages creative thinking and gives all employees space and time to innovate. Likewise, Toyota is known for its continuous improvement philosophy, and Accenture is recognized for its high-performance culture. These attributes live at the core of each company's employment brand, and have become a powerful part of its employer personality.

Another such example is Starbucks. As an employer, Starbucks prides itself on its employment promise. And the confidence to deliver a different job experience is reflected in the choice of words on Starbucks career centre website – 'For one thing, the people who work here aren't "employees" – we're 'partners' because we passionately share common goals and mutual success. We're dedicated to serving ethically sourced coffee, caring for the environment and giving back to the communities where we do business.'

Starbucks offers a 'partnership' experience, something the local neighbourhood coffee shop with the 'Help wanted' advert in the window cannot. That's what makes Starbucks different.

A universal framework

One of the best EVP models in the marketplace belongs to the US based think-tank, The Corporate Executive Board, which via its CLC Human Resources arm, has developed a simple framework to help organizations decode employment attributes.

According to the CLC model, an organization's employment promise is made up of five variables – rewards, opportunity, work, people and organization (as shown in Figure 5.2). A company's relative strength on each variable in turn influences how it should go about attracting and retaining talent.

FIGURE 5.2 The CLC model of an organization's employment value proposition

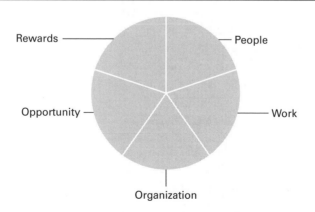

These five variables are in turn made up of 38 factors, as illustrated in Figure 5.3.

FIGURE 5.3 The factors making up the five variables in the CLC model of an organization's employment promise

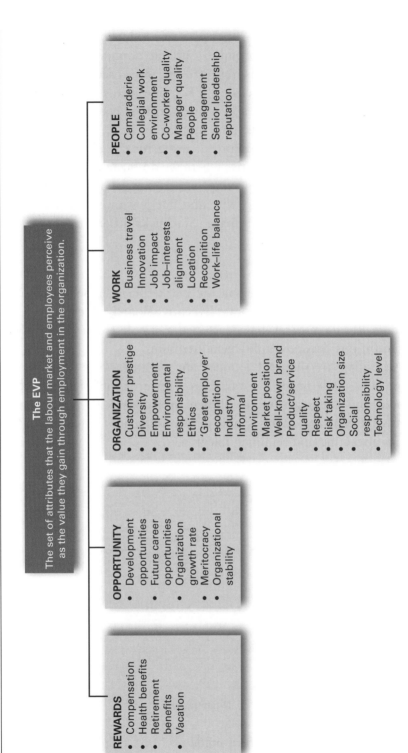

The EVP

The set of attributes that the labour market and employees perceive as the value they gain through employment in the organization.

REWARDS
- Compensation
- Health benefits
- Retirement benefits
- Vacation

OPPORTUNITY
- Development opportunities
- Future career opportunities
- Organization growth rate
- Meritocracy
- Organizational stability

ORGANIZATION
- Customer prestige
- Diversity
- Empowerment
- Environmental responsibility
- Ethics
- 'Great employer' recognition
- Industry
- Informal environment
- Market position
- Well-known brand
- Product/service quality
- Respect
- Risk taking
- Organization size
- Social responsibility
- Technology level

WORK
- Business travel
- Innovation
- Job impact
- Job-interests alignment
- Location
- Recognition
- Work-life balance

PEOPLE
- Camaraderie
- Collegial work environment
- Co-worker quality
- Manager quality
- People management
- Senior leadership reputation

SOURCE: The Corporate Executive Board, CLC Human Resources.

A good EVP is nothing but the recipe of value an organization promises a prospective employee, and the exact mix of that recipe can be found within the 38 variables of this model. By polling employees and candidates, it is possible to identify and rank which of these factors are areas of strength in a company and should form the core of a company's employment promise.

Great employers promise reality

But the promise is only one part of this equation. The other part is delivery. In other words, does the candidate experience the culture promised once he or she joins? This can only happen if your EVP promises reality ('this is who we are') rather than aspiration ('this is who we want to be').

To illustrate this point, here is one of the best examples of selling employment reality. It comes from 100 years ago, during the glory days of Antarctic exploration.

CASE STUDY A tale of endurance

Sir Ernest Shackleton wasn't the most famous Antarctic explorer of his generation. That honour would go to Major Robert Scott. He didn't win the intense race to the South Pole either. Norwegian Roald Amundsen got there first. However, in tough, crisis situations, it is Shackleton who is considered one of the greatest leaders of men.

A merchant mariner with a thirst for adventure, Shackleton joined and eventually led a number of exploration forays on the southern continent. On his third trip to the Antarctic, aiming to be the first expedition to cross the entire continent on foot, Shackleton and his crew of 27 men struck disaster. His ship, the Endurance, encountered unseasonable ice floes in the seas around Antarctica, which made it impossible to approach land. Eventually, the ship got stuck in thick ocean ice 80 miles short of land, leaving Shackleton and his crew no choice but to wait out the perilous winter months on board the frozen ship. Eight months later when the thaw began, the Endurance, which had been structurally damaged by shifting ocean ice, took on water and sank, forcing Shackleton to abandon ship and set up camp on the frozen ocean. Shackleton and his crew lived off the ice for another 14 months, before conditions allowed the group to set sail in two salvaged lifeboats towards the nearest civilization 800 miles away. Months later and after several failed attempts to traverse the world's most treacherous seas, Sir Ernest and his entire crew of 27 sailors reached safety.

In spite of spending two years in some of the most inhospitable, treacherous and life-threatening conditions, Shackleton hadn't lost a single crew member. In addition, most of his crew were in surprisingly good spirits when they returned. They put this down to one overriding factor – Shackleton's leadership.

Over the years, seeking to understand how Sir Ernest Shackleton and his crew survived impossible odds, historians and management gurus alike have studied and deconstructed Shackleton's management style and technique. What they found is that along with heaps of courage, he had a simple leadership philosophy and a similarly simple set of practices, many of which can be applied today to increasingly turbulent business environments.

In particular, Shackleton had an uncanny acumen for aligning his crew's expectations to reality at every stage of the expedition. In the same vein, his approach to attracting and hiring his crew before the expedition started demonstrated a sense of honesty and candour rarely seen in hiring practices today. When setting out to hire an expedition crew, Shackleton is fabled to have placed the following advert in the 'Men wanted' section of the London newspapers:

'MEN WANTED, for hazardous journey, small wages, bitter cold,
long months of complete darkness, constant danger, safe return doubtful.
Honour and recognition in case of success.'

Few leaders have the courage to say things as plainly as Shackleton chose to, and many would argue that this level of honesty would drive people away rather than attract them. Yet Shackleton's advert drew over 5,000 responses.

A year later, when stuck on the ice, his crew members stayed committed in spite of life threatening odds. They each contributed to keeping the next person alive, and trusted their leader's judgement implicitly. Much of Shackleton's success can be attributed to his emphasis on hiring crew members with the right perspective for the job. One can only imagine what could have happened if Shackleton had presented a slightly more complimentary reality to his future employees when hiring them.

Shackleton's story sets great context for selling reality to prospective employees. While this is a prerequisite, the best organizations take this a step further. They work hard at delivering an EVP that is closely aligned to their core CVP. Aligning your customer and employee brands as closely as possible has several advantages. The message is easier to believe, for one. In addition, if prospective employees have actually used a product and like it, they may view a job offer more favourably.

I have a personal example. Early in my management career I joined American Express purely because I was a fan of their efficiency and customer service. I trusted the Amex card more than any other in my wallet, and when a great job came my way, it was easy to join an organization I trusted anyway.

How the best companies do it

CASE STUDY   Apple and Samsung

Apple is a great example of a clearly aligned EVP. Apple as a company has always tried to think in different ways from its competition. In 1997, when Steve Jobs returned to lead the company again, Apple unveiled the 'Think different' advertising campaign. As much a statement to employees as it was to customers, this campaign not only helped revive the company's fortune but lay the foundation for all product innovation since. It isn't surprising then that the company's job adverts describe Apple as a place 'where you're encouraged to defy routine. To explore the far reaches of the possible.'

One of Apple's strongest competitors, Samsung, the Korean electronics giant, is a coveted employer in Asia and elsewhere in the world. In stark contrast to Apple's invitation for disruptive innovation, Samsung prefers to sell employees a promise of structured development and career planning. Here's what its careers website offers: 'A clear career path is plan(ned) for you when you join us and every effort is made to ensure a challenging and enriching career for you.' Not a bad strategy if you ask me. It clearly differentiates Samsung from the competition and reflects a starkly different people management culture.

In all the examples above we have seen companies promise a distinct experience to employees. Like Shackleton, they stand a good chance of attracting talent in the form of employees who will prosper at work – not merely cope.

As important as it is to promise reality, it is also equally important to ensure that misplaced promises don't inflate candidates' expectations, or attract those looking for experiences that cannot be delivered. For example, weeks after making thousands redundant across the world, one of the world's largest banks had the words 'If you thrive on challenges and recognition, XX Bank is the place for your career of a lifetime' on its recruitment website. While 'challenge and recognition' may well be very strong components of the bank's employment promise, seeing the words 'career' and 'lifetime' in the same sentence, I couldn't help but think of recent newspaper articles and television reports that had been saying quite the opposite.

An EVP makes financial sense too and research has shown that high-performing organizations are more likely to have a formal EVP in place than their industry peers (WorldatWork and Towers Watson, 2010). If your firm doesn't have a well-formulated and well-researched EVP, now may just be the best time to start. The war for talent in many global locations puts a premium on our ability to get the right attitude through the door and, equally, our ability to manage new employees' expectations. A good EVP, eventually, helps you do both.

> Note: The talent economics toolkit at the end of this book includes a detailed step-by-step checklist for those keen to publish an EVP for their organization.

Assimilating new talent

I have the fortune of sharing my time between two homes, in two different cities. One I have stayed in for over 40 years, while the other is relatively new – I have stayed there just over five years. The neighbourhoods are different too. One is made up of old neighbours. Most know each other well. We played together as kids, and now our children play together. And the rules of this community are now well set; there are unarticulated boundaries that allow us to coexist, share and thrive. As a result, relationships are strong. I know if I need help, there are at least five doors I can knock on instantly.

In the other city we live among predominantly floating residents. We've had three next door neighbours over the last five years, including one with a penchant for loud music just when our light-sleeping younger child was still toddling. When we hang out at the community pool or gym there always seem to be new faces around. As a result, our friendships are superficial, and in spite of notice boards full of rules, I see many unwittingly (or knowingly) flout them.

In many ways organizations, beyond the structure and organization charts, are communities. And whether they want to, or not, communities share a common ethos – a collective character. In a neighbourhood, this character is diffused, because all we want to do is coexist peacefully through a mix of good manners, friendship, helpfulness and fun. But in commercial situations, we also need a willingness to win – to be better than the competition – and we need interdependence – the ability to contribute to each other's success. It is in these two areas that a strong corporate culture can be a powerful instrument.

If the study of corporate culture has a predominant guru, it would be Edgar H Schein, Professor Emeritus at MIT. Schein, who has studied the elements of culture for over half a century has a simple three-layer model for understanding corporate culture (Schein, 2009). The three levels are:

- **Artefacts.** These are made up of visible structures, processes and behaviour. Easy to observe, artefacts are the outermost layer.

- **Espoused values.** These are the strategies and philosophies at play. They include what people focus on and 'how things get done around here'.

- **Underlying assumptions.** These are the unconscious beliefs and perceptions rooted in the history of the business. This innermost layer is built through collective experiences including past successes and failures.

Corporate culture is as powerful as it is multifaceted. The best way to understand it is to experience it first hand. Be immersed in both the explicit behaviour and implicit beliefs. And it is through culture that each organization gives meaning to leadership.

Vineet Nayar at HCL taught us that culture can be deliberately managed and changed, when he turned his company around using the simple EFCS (employee first, customer second) philosophy (see Chapter 2). But unless you have a leader like Nayar, the CEO is probably the last person to ask for a candid assessment of his or her company's culture – that is, unless you are looking for a half-hour monologue on everything from values to strategy. Instead, seek out a middle manager who joined the company exactly 12 months ago. In this time, he or she would have gathered enough personal experience and evidence to share an early hypothesis on each of Schein's three levels – how people behave, what is the dominant management philosophy, and what people believe to be true.

As this manager talks about his or her experiences, enumerates examples or details stories, you will also notice something else. After spending a year assimilating into this new cultural fabric, he or she will appear either energized or defeated.

Helping new employees (at all levels) succeed is one of the strongest levers you have to improve your organization and its culture over time. It's logical. New hires are empty slates, and hence much more impressionable and influenced than the 10-year company veteran.

New employees also have heaps of incentive. No one joins a company to fail. All new hires want to succeed and hence value every opportunity and assistance to do so.

Typically, every new hire you make goes through the same five-stage assimilation process, which looks something like Figure 5.4.

FIGURE 5.4   The five stages of assimilation

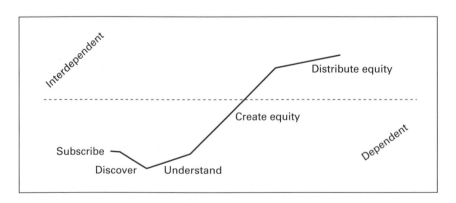

If I were a new employee joining a new company here's how I would experience the five stages:

- **Subscription.** All employment relationships start here. I need to make a commitment and turn up. I would typically be feeling excited; my adrenaline would be pumping, but my enthusiasm is laced with a shade of trepidation.

- **Discover.** I go through my first few weeks learning on overdrive. Each day seems like a breakthrough. I gather my first experiences and clarify my assumptions. I am starting to discover the culture of this new workplace. I also meet lots of new people and go through strong emotions such as validation, inclusion, insight and even some disappointment.

- **Understand.** In a few months, I get into a familiar rhythm. I set some personal rules and start to codify how I can be successful here. The rulebook is now clear and I am able to interpret this organization's culture through every experience. I start forming an early coalition outside my direct team and I am feeling more confident.

- **Create equity.** I am now ready to put my own ideas and strategy into play. There is so much we can improve here. My first successes give me energy to take bigger risks. By now I have built strong alliances through the firm by finding people I can rely on and call upon for advice. My energy levels are high, as are my hopes for success.

- **Distribute equity.** By now, I see the bigger picture and discover new opportunities to contribute, even if indirectly. I know my thoughts and contribution are valued and I feel less insecure about my personal success. I have gathered a sense of wisdom about how to be successful here and am willing to share this with others.

Almost everyone goes through a similar cycle. In some places it could take months, in others several years to arrive at stage five. A lot of factors matter, including how new employees are managed, their ability to develop the right skills at the right time and the coaching they receive. But most of all, they need an enabling culture that is oriented towards employees' empowerment and success.

A lot can go wrong during the five stages. Let's say the culture cannot sustain new ideas, or a direct manager doesn't support equity development. Then the curve you see in Figure 5.4 could flatten prematurely while the employee still feels dependent.

Without a chance to feel interdependent and secure, in a while, the employee may choose to physically quit and leave. Even more tragically the person might mentally quit, and stay.

2. Build unconventional entry points for talent

To buy or build? That is the question

Organizations have traditionally used a couple of hiring strategies to bring in fresh talent. Some hire large cohorts of young interns and trainees straight from college campuses and then invest considerable time and energy in helping this talent grow in the company. Building talent from the bottom up is a slow process and requires significant foresight into the organization's future talent needs.

The buy approach is the exact opposite. Organizations that prefer predominantly to buy talent look to fill vacancies by attracting experienced talent from the marketplace, often from similar roles in other companies. Buying talent is faster, and allows an organization to add capability it may not possess internally. It is also the preferred strategy when an organization needs to increase scale rapidly.

The vast majority of global businesses, in practice, use a highly customized mix of both buy and build strategies to get fresh talent in the door. This makes sense. Building talent is proactive and long term. Buying is reactive and short term. This recipe has worked for decades.

Yet the most innovative firms are now looking to break these moulds, or at a minimum, stretch them beyond their conventional definitions, because social conventions themselves are changing. For one, we increasingly live in an age of non-linear careers. Employees don't necessarily only aspire to the role their boss holds, they aspire in all directions. For another, there is less social stigma associated with job losses, career shifts or even 'downshifting' to a more junior role.

Values are changing too. Employees increasingly seek more meaning from work, or choose work–life balance over seniority or money.

Younger employees exemplify this best. Many young graduates are consciously choosing non-conventional careers or opting to flit more casually between entrepreneurship, portfolio careers and corporate roles. **The reality is that careers increasingly come with a reboot button, and companies that realize this early possess a competitive talent advantage.** This means we must be willing to explore the talent jungle beyond the well-trodden campus and lateral hiring routes. Here are some ideas.

Mid-career internships

As an example, one unconventional hiring method in early experimentation is mid-career internships. Involving nothing more complicated than taking the entry level internship model further up the hierarchy, mid-career internships allow mature talent a unique low obligation entry point.

Victor Hugo said: 'Nothing is more powerful than an idea whose time has come.' I feel this is one idea that will define not just job mobility but career mobility in the 21st century. In my role as an executive coach, I frequently come across people who feel stuck in a current job. When I ask them why they feel that way, the answers range from external factors such as 'Technology is taking over, and shrinking the trade as a whole' to personal factors, for example 'To be honest, after 17 years of doing this, I'm bored – I've lost my mojo.'

Most of my interviewees have some idea of what else they would like to do. Some want to transfer to a different function in their existing organizations, while others want to make a clean start in a different environment; but this isn't always possible. Invariably they have families to support, or are in middle management or senior functional roles and don't want to take a serious career dive back to the bottom of the pyramid. They shouldn't have to either, as many possess valuable management experience, or have dealt with customers or managed successful business operations. They bring strong transferable skills, yet crave an inspiring new experience. The traditional buy and build recruitment models have no interest in this request. Smart companies who are willing to open this door, and invest a little in building proficiency, can gain access to some serious talent.

There is a great example emerging out of Asia.

CASE STUDY An example – Private banks in Asia

With the shift of global wealth eastwards, the number of millionaires in Asia has been growing at an impressive clip. According to leading Swiss private bank Julius Baer, Asia's group of 'high net worth individuals' is set to more than double within the next five years (Julius Baer/CLSA, 2011). And it isn't just India and China where numbers are rising. The fastest growing market is, in fact, Indonesia.

As a direct consequence of this growth, every major bank in the region is looking to bolster its private banking teams by hiring more wealth managers. But wealth managers are in short supply, and it takes years to grow them from the bottom up. Clients are only willing to entrust their millions to mature and well-heeled wealth managers, not a 22-year-old associate.

Faced with an acute shortage of talent, at least one bank in the region has already started experimenting with hiring professionals, for example doctors or lawyers, as mid-career interns and then investing in developing their financial skills. The experiment is working. I met one, a doctor, who had started feeling claustrophobic in his small family clinic and hence pressed the career reboot button. While he had a lot to learn about financial products, a background in medicine made him very comfortable with diagnosis and giving advice. In addition, over an 18-year career, he had dealt and built lasting relationships with countless affluent patients. These are priceless skills.

I think we will see more and more such examples in the future. By 2020, mid-career shifts will be a more common reality, and the really smart organizations will have well-established programmes to retool mature interns.

Returnships

A returnship is another example of a mid-career internship with one defining difference. It is aimed at those seeking re-employment after an extended career break, particularly women. In Chapter 4 we saw that increasing the participation rate of women at the workplace will prove critical for many ageing economies. Everywhere we look, we see talented and well-qualified women who have chosen to stall their careers mid-stream, in most cases to start or nurture a young family. After a few years, many want to return to their career, but struggle to find a foothold back on the right rung of the career ladder.

A few years off can be very disorienting, and result in a loss of confidence or context. This is why returnees need high-quality transition support to make a successful return, be it formal mentoring or refresher courses in business management or updates on technology at the workplace.

The first formal returnship programmes on record were offered by the Sara Lee Corporation and by Goldman Sachs in 2008. At Sara Lee in particular, this was championed at the very top. CEO Brenda Barnes had herself taken a break earlier in her career at PepsiCo to spend more time with her family, and then made a successful return. Commenting on why the Sara Lee programme serves as an important example, Barnes says: 'There's this huge pool of talent out there, of women who have decided to take time off for family reasons and have a hard time coming back... They didn't lose their brains when they left the workforce, yet... their confidence levels aren't as high as they should be' (reported in an article entitled 'Sara Lee Launches "Returnship" Program for On-Rampers' and published in the *Wall Street Journal* blog on 23 October 2008).

Returnships aren't just for women. Indeed, they work equally well for both genders. But if your goal is to increase the representation of women at the very top of your organization in the future, opening doors for returning female talent at middle-management level could prove a massive leap in the right direction.

Farm your alumni

The Corporate Alumni programme is another idea gaining speed. An unfortunate reality of ever-increasing career mobility is that every company today also has an ever-increasing pool of ex-employees. And while it is easy to collect an access card and close affairs with a final pay cheque, the relationship often doesn't end there. Each ex-employee remains an ambassador, with valuable institutional knowledge and ongoing personal relationships.

Until a few years ago, companies had no means to keep this relationship alive. Tracking alumni movement was administratively daunting; and fostering physical networks was expensive and time consuming. Further, alumni clubs have been the traditional reserve of academic institutions, which invest deeply in keeping ex-students connected, primarily because they are a lucrative source for funding. Then things changed. Companies started accepting their alumni as a powerful and useful demographic. Professional services went first, with consulting companies such as McKinsey recognizing that successful alumni were also potential clients. Today corporate alumni networks are on a hot streak. The arrival of online networking platforms such as LinkedIn or MySpace have suddenly made alumni networking relatively easier and infinitely more efficient. Ex-employee networks are thus emerging as valuable channels of talent across a broader set of companies. Alumni are a great audience for open job advertisements. They understand the cultural DNA better than an absolutely raw candidate, and may already possess an internal network to rely on.

Open source talent

The big game changer, however, will be resourcing models that make the organization's boundaries more porous to external talent, ie creating an outside-in resourcing system. The best examples – Open and Crowd Sourcing – are already revolutionizing the technology world. We can see it everywhere, from Amazon to Wikipedia.

CASE STUDY

At Mozilla, developers of the world's most popular internet browser, Firefox, the company itself is a large open sourced project, relying extensively on outside-in innovation. Over 40 per cent of the code at Mozilla is contributed by volunteers (Finette, 2010).

The last decade has seen many companies from more traditional industries develop their own external capability sourcing model. In Chapter 2 we saw how Procter & Gamble (P&G) uses external talent on a number of R&D projects. Through its 'Connect & Develop' platform, P&G's research and innovation projects reach well beyond its own captive R&D team to potentially millions of scientists, developers and researchers in all corners of the world. Forming teams made up of internal R&D employees and external talent, the company keeps a tight leash on development, yet allows for critical outside-in contribution. It's a win–win like no other. P&G gets access to the best minds, and external talent gets an opportunity to work with a market leader like P&G.

Open source resourcing is catching on like wildfire, yet there isn't one universal template. Each industry and company must discover an independent approach. One thing is certain, as with the other talent attraction trends above, inventing an approach is always better than playing catch-up.

3. Poach your talent before the competition does

Build bridges, not walls

Like people, organizations have a lifecycle. Most start small, flexible and full of ideas. Those that are successful invariably grow in size and scale, which also means they invariably need greater structure. It could be in the form of specializations, territories, business units and other mechanisms of distributed accountability. Even in the leanest and most hi-tech of firms, increases in scale invariably lead to increases in structure. Yet structure, for all its virtue and efficiency, is also prone to a chronic disease – fragmentation.

In theory, a firm should have no internal boundaries. The lines of an organization chart should merely represent exactly that – a system of organization. But often they become much more. Unless companies are very careful, the lines can easily become walls, giving rise to divisive practices such as silo thinking and fiefdoms.

Fragmentation is a toxic state. It slows down information sharing, breeds redundancy and distracts employees from focusing on the only two people who should really matter – the customer and shareholder. And it can devastate a firm's ability to manage its talent. How? One of the clearest symptoms of a fragmented organization is when talented individuals struggle to see (and sometimes even seek) career opportunities beyond their immediate environment.

Here's one example.

CASE STUDY

I was quite surprised when a smart young graduate I knew informed me of her decision to move on from the blue chip firm she had been so desperate to join just a few years earlier. Concerned that she might be making a mistake, I decided to pick up the phone and find out why. It turned out that her interest in finance, her career choice after completing an MBA, had waned, and she was keen to move into marketing. I actually found her reasons to do so quite sound – a desire to be closer to customers being one of them. Yet she had found it impossible to gain any momentum to move within her existing firm. Everyone, from her manager to HR personnel had offered her more reasons why a switch would be difficult than suggestions on next steps. 'I love my company but, eventually,' she said, 'I found it easier to find a job outside.'

This isn't a stray incident. In theory, talent belongs to the company as a whole, and not to functions or subdivisions. But in practice, the more disconnected the firm, the tougher it is for employees to access career opportunities from within.

Your internal mobility index

We know that 21st-century employees are more mobile and possess a broader career viewpoint than employees in the past. In an employment era such as the one upon us, this makes internal mobility a virtue. It is also a measure of an organization's health. Losing good people because we were not able to accommodate a 'reasonable' desire for career or geographic mobility is nothing but poor management.

To see how geared your organization is, ask yourself the following questions:

- Do you have a robust mobility policy; specifying eligibility and process?
- Is it freely shared with all employees?

- Are all open roles advertised internally first?
- Is internal talent preferred when compared to external hires? How is this enforced?
- Do you track and analyse internal mobility?
- Are internal hiring statistics shared with senior managers?
- How do you encourage internal mobility? For example, do you share success stories of internal moves?
- Do employees have access to career counselling? Is this freely advertised and used?
- Are managers encouraged to have an annual career discussion with their direct reports? How many do?
- Are you happy with the following ratio (measured on an annual basis per 100 employees) within your firm?
  Internal mobility : external hires : resignations

There is no silver bullet ratio for the last question, though you will instantaneously know which of the three dials is not in tune. To improve this ratio, you must first create the circumstances for mobility:

- Visibly encourage internal mobility.
- Encourage career experimentation.
- Build confidence in employees to share their career aspirations with their managers.
- Offer avenues for career counselling.
- Ensure that all employees have a view of all open roles and set common ground rules for application and hiring.

Especially if you are an industry leader, remember this is an imperative, not an option. Poaching from within is a much better outcome than having your competition poach your precious talent.

4. Create an expansive mindset

'*If the doors of perception were cleansed every thing would appear to man as it is, infinite. For man has closed himself up, till he sees all things through narrow chinks of his cavern.*' **WILLIAM BLAKE, *THE MARRIAGE OF HEAVEN AND HELL***

I often encounter managers who seek to hire in their own reflection. I can understand the way they think. It's easy to derive a sense of comfort or confidence from a similar background. At a personal level, hiring someone who went to the same college or has a similar career path can even seem less risky as a decision.

Most people don't have a full grasp on their recruitment predispositions. But we all have them. And they show themselves in the recruitment profiles we write or in the choice of interview questions or how we make a hiring decision. This is the exact problem with bias – it is often unconscious. Because unconscious bias enters the decision process disguised as a hunch, or something your gut tells you, it can be difficult to notice or identify.

Yet evidence of its impact is all around us – in managers insisting on college education, when a role doesn't necessarily require it; in promotion criteria that prefer minimum tenures over demonstrated competence; or in campus hiring where organizations seek to screen talented future stars via a standard profile of academic scores. This is an endemic issue. At a time when organizations are struggling to find high-quality talent, the question to ask is: **Is there truly a shortage of talent or are our hiring templates too restrictive?**

Eliminate unconscious bias

A good place to start is to look at the way job descriptions (and job specifications) are used in the hiring process. I love job descriptions. They are a great way of communicating how a role fits into a team and what an employee must focus on. Job descriptions are also an important part of selling the reality of the job. But they must only and always be based on very strong job analysis, which preferably should be done by a neutral and qualified expert. If not, they run the serious risk of blurring needs with preferences. Too often we find managers writing or adapting job descriptions or job specifications without the necessary professional input. Ask yourself if that 'five years of similar work experience' really is a must. Likewise, how does a college degree earned 15 years ago stack up against strong transferable skills exhibited more recently?

Over time, a restrictive approach to background or experience can severely hamper our efforts to find the right employees. In reality though, every recruitment mandate is a golden opportunity to broaden a team's diversity.

Traditionally, diversity efforts have focused on achieving an equitable demographic mix based on gender, race or age. In the future though, with increasing business ambiguity, the focus must also be on achieving diversity of experiences, backgrounds and thought. The aim is to broaden our pool of potential talent and actively look for diversity in hiring. The only way you can do this is by recasting both your recruitment mindset and method. Start by looking at job descriptions and filters for candidate selection for any signs of unsubstantiated criteria. Broaden the efforts to source employees: look in new places. Next, make the pool of interviewers more diverse by getting neutral peers involved in selection.

In short, look for and reassess every 'sacred cow' criteria or practice. Increasing the scope of hiring does two things: it brings more options to the table, and it challenges managers to think differently.

5. Open the window – think outside-in

In Chapter 1 we discussed how much the basic tenets of employment have changed over a mere 30 years. Let's recap some key points:

- Retirement is no longer an integral part of the employer–employee dialogue.
- Job security is loosely implicit for only the top 15 or 20 per cent of the workforce, and that too isn't recession proof.
- Benefits are no longer just hygiene factors and are getting increasingly monetized.
- Most importantly, with career flexibility the norm and shorter attention spans all around, the stigma associated with job hopping is rapidly fading.

Another force set to reshape the 21st century employment equation is the rapidly growing quantity of outside-in intelligence on a company, freely available over the internet. Apart from making both candidates and current employees better informed than ever before, the availability of what used to be confidential information is already proving very tricky for employers.

Earlier in this chapter I spoke about companies crafting and communicating a realistic EVP at the core of their recruitment efforts, something that roughly one third of large companies have already done. Whether you have a formal EVP or not, you shouldn't be surprised that your colleagues have already written an informal one for you.

Since 2007 sites such as Glassdoor.com, WetFeet.com and Vault. com, among others, have been collecting and compiling employee and ex-employee perceptions of your firm. Armed with thousands of individual experiences, these sites have now started to create intricate profiles and rankings all available on your desktop, for free. The data you can amass on thousands of employers is simply astonishing, and is multiplying with every passing day. Companies that haven't started thinking about how this will have an impact on them risk waking up in a few years feeling more than a little exposed. It will be quite like a 21st-century, digital-age adaptation of the popular Hans Christian Andersen fable *The Emperor's New Clothes*.

Why? Because candid employment experiences are only the start. In the days ahead, access to more sensitive data can make management a very tricky proposition. A prime example is the growth of outside-in compensation intelligence.

From privileged intelligence

For the better part of 40 years, compensation benchmarking was HR's Holy Grail. By investing in expensive research benchmarking annual salaries, compensation managers had great decision power, a bird's-eye view of the pay and benefits market. Have salaries gone up, or down? Which jobs were in greater demand? How should salary budgets change? These were all questions HR had the power to answer, given its general insight to trends.

Salary benchmarking data is highly customized and confidential and this is a fact that makes it privileged information, even within a senior management team. It is also very expensive, and a medium-sized firm can easily spend a few hundred thousand dollars a year to gain an insight into market compensation intelligence.

To open intelligence

But the game has changed rapidly since the start of this millennium. In an age where careers are more unstructured and salary expectations less calibrated across the world, these bulky surveys are getting increasingly peripheral. Here are a couple of symptoms of this shift.

As recent as 10 years ago, an employee had limited opportunity to benchmark his of her value. Even if nursing a nagging suspicion of not being paid fairly, employees had but a limited network of friends and relatives to reach out to. To make matters worse, pay scales weren't the easiest of subjects to discuss socially.

The internet changed all that, and in came Payscale.com, Salary. com, BMMP.com (BenchMarkMyPay), and a dozen more salary benchmarking sites. These are changing the game and growing more sophisticated with every passing year.

Today, in a few short minutes and for as little as under a hundred dollars, a highly personalized, professional, illustrated, personally benchmarked salary survey sits on every employee's desktop. These sites have millions of salary inputs, put in by single users like you and me. How much does an average web designer in Shanghai get paid? In response, over 200 inputs exist. What about a PE analyst in San Francisco? How about 300 data points on this one?

HR departments paying hundreds of thousands of dollars for surveys are in a quandary. Employees and candidates have started bringing some strong market intelligence to the bargaining table.

One candidate interviewing for a role recently e-mailed graphs back to the recruiter backing up an expected salary number. Another young candidate seeking to join a major hotel chain posted a simple question to his social network: 'How much do you think a front desk supervisor at this hotel should get paid?' Within days he had 36 responses and had been forward networked to four people who had worked there. His prophetic words when we met a few months later were: 'I knew more about what I was worth than the recruiter who made me the offer.'

Talent, just like gold or any other precious commodity, is subject to the same demand and supply economics.

Pay information is one of many examples that highlight the need for organizations to be more reverse engineered and externally focused. Market intelligence is the name of game, and for the first time in history, it is in the hands of the average employee.

True equity

The whole concept of pay benchmarking itself comes from the studies by John Stacey Adams on workplace equity in the mid-1960s. Adam's equity theory simply states that workers feel valued and fairly dealt with based on three specific variables:

- the workers' own contribution;
- the benefit received in exchange for contribution;
- how they are being treated relative to others doing comparable jobs (ie whether their peers get a similar benefit for a similar contribution).

If employees perceive all three variables are in balance, they are motivated to perform. If on the other hand, they suspect they are receiving less benefit or being asked to work harder than colleagues, they will be motivated to act on their perception of inequity, either by complaining or by wilfully reducing their contribution.

For all its simplicity, the concept of equity is one of the foundational canons of the employment agreement. When employees feel underpaid or overworked compared to their peers, it destroys much more than productivity. It damages trust.

Today, the responsibility for benchmarking contribution and pay lies with the HR department, which invests considerable effort in ensuring equity across large employee populations. In the future though, with employees increasingly benchmarking relative contribution and pay with a broader external audience, our ability to deal with episodes of perceived inequity have to get better. One way is to empower managers to have a more transparent dialogue with an employee. Another is to communicate pay ranges and externally validated market data to all employees, thereby building trust and negating outside influences.

Adams said in 1965 that employees who perceive inequity or feel undervalued are motivated to act, either by reducing performance or complaining. In today's environment of high mobility, it is only the average performer who chooses to drop contribution and stay. The best performers won't consider this option. Many won't complain either. They will go seeking someone who values them more.

6. Help innovation thrive – create organizational flow

Think granular innovation rather than process adherence

We know that the great 20th-century organizations became great through process. They worked hard at achieving standardization, incrementally improving quality. They tweaked and tuned every subcomponent until it was perfect. Quality stood out, and in most cases better quality was in itself a competitive advantage. But then, the 20th century was a 'manufacturing' century.

The great organizations of the 21st century will be built on flow. For the 21st century is an 'innovation' century. Consider this quote by Kevin Kelly, who co-founded *Wired* magazine: 'Wealth in this new regime flows directly from innovation, not optimization; that is, wealth is not gained by perfecting the known, but by imperfectly seizing the unknown.'

This is the new reality. The 'quality revolution' in the latter half of the 20th century has taken us to a point where all products that reach a supermarket shelf work. Most do what they are meant to do quite well. The competitive differentiators of the future will be products that are the most innovative, even though they may not be the best.

Anyone standing in the mile-long queue I saw on a London curb in June 2010 would agree. Some had stood in that queue overnight – to buy the latest iPhone. Flawed antenna, dropped calls, shattering glass notwithstanding; they wanted the latest product, and they wanted it before everyone else. In this instance, over one and a half million iphone4s were sold on the first day of launch. Welcome to 21st-century flow.

Flow

Flow grows from a foundation of improvement and mastery. Mihaly Csikszentmihalyi, the University of Chicago Professor who created the concept in 1972, describes it as 'a state of experience, when we are totally involved in what we are doing' (Csikszentmihalyi, 1990).

Individuals can be in flow. Great artists, creators and leaders achieve it regularly, when time melts away in pursuit of a goal, and all capabilities at their disposal are acutely focused on the task at hand. In the same vein organizations can be in flow too, by pursuing clear goals with collective energy. Organizational flow is nothing but a shift of aggregate employee focus from constraints and impediments to possibilities.

Achieving flow, both for individuals and groups, can be a powerful and heady experience. It isn't achieved by eliminating distractions or creating the perfect environment or culture. On the contrary, it is achieved in spite of distractions. And it is deliberate. Organizational flow is a deliberate and direct outcome of visible single-minded focus in a senior management team, ie leaders with a compelling vision and the ability to inspire the same vision in others.

There are three additional ingredients needed to achieve a purposeful and innovative flow organization in the 21st century. These are the right competencies, the right environment and the right incentives to drive innovation.

FIGURE 5.5   Creating organizational flow

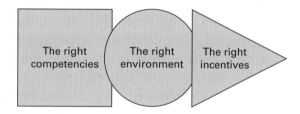

The **right competencies** are the mindset and 'skillset' to thrive in a faster paced world. These include:

- The courage and ability to challenge convention and to innovate. In other words, this means learning agility, achievement orientation and, most importantly, the willingness to take risks. Not all employees need to be 'ideators', but we need a critical mass – just enough to drive sustainable innovation. And we need them in the right roles.

- The ability to see the big picture. In a globally connected world, competition can come from anywhere. Middle managers and frontline staff closest to the customer get a sense of market momentum weeks before data can reach senior managers. The stronger the conversation between these levels, the greater the ability to spot the next big trend.

- The willingness to collaborate. In my opinion this is probably the most important competence for the future. Complexity in business has evolved faster than human ability. Our only hedge is to pool resources and play to each other's strengths.

The **right environment** is one of trust:

- It is an environment where mistakes can be made and where leaders encourage experimentation and lateral thinking.
- Most of all it features a workplace that is relaxed and informal, without dysfunctional relationships and bureaucracy.
- Silo thinking in particular can have devastating consequences on organizational flow. It leads to compartmentalization of critical knowledge, hinders collaboration and almost always denies people the opportunity to see the big picture. For organizations to bring interdisciplinary wisdom to the table, silo thinking must go. People must also feel comfortable challenging fundamental assumptions or 'holy cows' without being considered crazy.

The following case study illustrates what we don't want.

CASE STUDY

Many people know that Kodak went out of business recently, after years of misery and decline, basically because the company misread the shift from photographic film to digital photography. But what most people don't know is that, in 1975, it was in fact Kodak that invented the first digital camera. The team at Kodak had a head start, the competence and the best minds. They owned the photography business. So much so that the perfect picture opportunity was universally called 'The Kodak Moment'.

Then why did Kodak fail, making wrong turn after wrong turn for 30 years until it finally reached the corporate graveyard?

Film was Kodak's holy 'cash' cow. Kodak dominated the global film business for decades, and enjoyed a 90 per cent market share in the United States. As a product it was also so profitable that at one point in time Kodak enjoyed a profit margin of 80 per cent on sales. Kodak's leaders, R&D teams and sales people were so attached to film that they refused to acknowledge warning signs, even when they were in plain sight.

Finally, the **right incentives** are needed and, I hasten to add, they are of both the monetary and non-monetary kind. These days, we find more and more companies using monetary incentives to drive performance, often to disastrous consequences. Aristotle concluded 2,300 years ago that more than anything, man seeks happiness; a maxim that still rings true today. I am not saying money is not important. Indeed it is virtually impossible for me to happy in a job if I nurse a nagging suspicion that I am not being paid fairly. But using mainly monetary incentives to motivate performance or innovation often proves counterproductive. Studies have shown, as Daniel Pink tells us in his revolutionary book *Drive*, more money can sometimes lead to inferior performance – because of increased performance pressure (Pink, 2009).

In other words, what we need is a reward system that pays people fairly, not one that makes 'increasing personal gain' the sole focus of performance. There is one exception, though, where a carrot (incentive) and stick (disincentive) approach does work, and that is when employees are involved in doing simple repetitive tasks, for example, in assembly line production.

For roles that require cognitive decision making, or taking risks, and when we want to foster true experimentation, non-monetary incentives work better; because, as Pink tells us, they help increase (and sustain) an employee's 'intrinsic motivation'.

Cash or non-cash?

A recent engagement study (CLC Human Resources Executive Board, 2009) looked at both the impact and decay rate of cash versus non-cash awards. This is what the survey found.

Cash awards (such as bonuses) were able to increase employees' engagement by around 8 per cent in the month immediately following payout. And this spike in engagement lingered. Six months later, engagement levels stayed 6 per cent higher than what they were before the payout. This makes common sense. Distributing a bonus is all about linking an organization's success with personal success and makes employees feel their contribution has been recognized.

The study also focused on the impact non-cash awards such as public recognition, certificates of achievement or 'thank you' notes had on an employees' overall engagement. It found that receiving a non-cash award actually increased engagement by over 9 per cent, well over what cash could achieve. But non-cash awards decay faster. Six months later the residual impact was between 4 and 5 per cent.

These are fascinating insights! Non-cash rewards have a greater impact, partly because they aren't as predictable as the long run-up to bonus day. They feel more legitimate and more authentic. They are cost effective too. On the flip side, non-cash awards depreciate faster, hence they cannot work if managers chose to use them once in a blue moon. Our goal instead should be to find a good balance between cash and non-cash incentives, and more importantly focus on getting the frequency right. This can help build and sustain the high levels of engagement needed to sustain innovation.

Innovation incentives

In addition to the mechanisms of 'overt' recognition we have just discussed, stepping up organizational flow also needs what I call 'innovation incentives'. The most important of these are time, space and freedom to experiment.

CASE STUDY What not to do!

I once interviewed a leader who believed that the purpose of his role was to keep his team busy all the time. 'Keeping them challenged' he called it. If someone had spare time, that person was a prime candidate for either a 'double hat' or a restructuring list.

'So where is the time for employees to think?' I asked him? He replied, 'Well, there's always the lunch hour.' Right.

This is more common than we think. Look around you at how many people have a majority of their day consumed by routine, be it mountains of e-mail, meaningless reports, daily meetings or conference calls.

The modern workplace is chaotic, fast paced and unpredictable. The answer is not to slow it down, but to create an emphasis on idea creation and experimentation. Replace some of the noise in your team's schedule with a stretch goal or two. This is relatively simple. Ask yourself whether employees around you are expected to share ideas regularly. Do you give them the platform to brainstorm or build momentum for these ideas? Do they have the bandwidth to experiment? Recent research tells us this isn't happening enough. When asked to agree or disagree with the statement: 'I feel empowered to offer ideas to improve my organization's outcomes' 6 out of 10 workers disagreed (CLC Human Resources Executive Board, 2009) .

Giving employees the space and time to innovate is a powerful incentive. It gives them purpose backed by means; it gives a reason to seek happiness at work. So what creates happiness? Pink tells us that there are three things that grow intrinsic motivation: purpose, mastery and autonomy.

The 21st-century 'flow organization' has few boundaries, is flexible and puts a premium on broad-based innovation. And we build it by not just engaging employees to work, but engaging their ideas as well. But how do we measure this? We do it through 'cerebral engagement'.

7. Measure and grow cerebral engagement

I am a huge fan of the employee engagement survey. This is principally because it gives us a true sense of an organization's current temperament.

Over the last 20 years, employee surveys have undergone a sea change both in popularity and sophistication. Led by companies such as Gallup, Hay, Mercer and others, the quality of analysis available today has sparked immense board-level interest in measuring and benchmarking employees' engagement levels.

Traditional employee surveys have tended to use a mix of **emotive and rational lenses** to view, analyse and report the health of a workforce.

Among other things, **emotive lenses** measure and clarify:

- Employees' overall satisfaction with work. How happy are they?
- Employees' pride in belonging. Are they proud to tell others where they work? Do they recommend their employer to others?

- Employees' empowerment. How trusted and valued do employees feel? Is there a collegiate environment at work?

- Social factors. Do employees have friends at work? Is the atmosphere friendly, conducive and comfortable?

On the other hand, **rational lenses** have traditionally looked at:

- Employees' commitment – their desire to leave or stay, normally over a defined period, for example two years.

- Employees' enablement. How supported do employees feel at work? Do they have the right tools and resources to perform?

- Discretionary effort. Do employees go above and beyond the basic requirements of their role?

Both emotive and rational lenses are critically essential in gauging employees' engagement. In practice, they are analogous to an annual health check, because they have the potential to prompt both proactive and preventive action.

But when we come to flow organization, traditional rational and emotive measures built in the last century (figure 5.6) tend to paint only part of the picture. The 21st-century organization needs an additional measure of insight. It needs a **cerebral engagement** measure.

Cerebral engagement is all about flow – the flow of ideas and innovation. Are employees learning while doing? Do they bring ideas to work and share them with others? Are they willing to defend their ideas against criticism? Do they thrive on change and are they looking to innovate?

Specifically, there are 10 statements that help map flow and cerebral engagement at work. I call them the CE10:

- I have ideas on how our company can improve its products or delivery to customers.

- I feel confident sharing and debating these ideas with my manager and other senior colleagues.

- My job directly contributes to my organization's success.

- My job is intellectually rewarding.

- I have regular opportunities to learn new skills 'on the job'.

- I actively track developments in our industry and what our competitors are doing.

- My goals motivate and challenge me.

FIGURE 5.6   Cerebral engagement

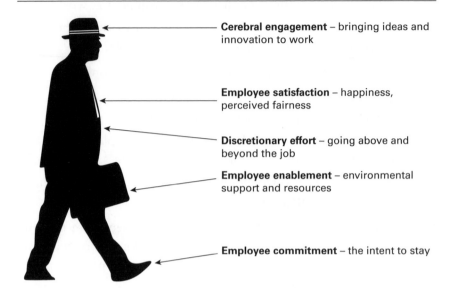

Cerebral engagement – bringing ideas and innovation to work

Employee satisfaction – happiness, perceived fairness

Discretionary effort – going above and beyond the job

Employee enablement – environmental support and resources

Employee commitment – the intent to stay

- I have the opportunity to collaborate with others on implementing new ideas.
- I don't feel afraid to make a mistake when trying something new.
- I see my manager primarily as my coach.

By polling employees we can begin to map our current circumstances for innovation. Find out how your company stacks up on the CE10. This is the clearest indicator of organizational flow in your firm. Does it work better in some parts of your company than others? Where are the innovation hotspots, as opposed to the bottlenecks? What can you do about them?

Both cerebral engagement and increasing flow are integral components of your company's talent strategy. Later in this book we examine approaches to prioritize and invest in generating organizational flow. Measurement is the first step.

21st-century talent strategy

06

This book has been written using three distinct lenses. Each lens has helped us look at talent from a graduated vantage point.

The early chapters focused a telescope on the rapidly changing realities of global business. By understanding how economies and businesses are adapting to an increasingly interdependent world, our aim was to look over the horizon – to what our world in 2020 may look like.

We then traded in the telescope for a magnifying glass. Our aim was to gain a closer view and study the ebb and flow of a 3-billion-strong, yet intricately nuanced, global workforce. This lens gave us the means to distinguish risks, opportunities and challenges across a spectrum of countries, and then look for similarities or differences in the geographies that matter to us. How does Poland compare with Australia? What will India's demographic dividend look like? Or for that matter, what will Russia's 'demographic discount' look like?

And finally, over the last few chapters we handed in the magnifying glass for a finely calibrated microscope, which could focus on the individual. By glancing into the mind of the 21st-century employee, we could study the changing employment equation and discover new ways to attract, motivate, and manage this new workforce.

So what?

Once the facts are neatly laid out, every business book eventually faces a 'so what?' question. What do we do with all this? How will it help me do my job better? It is now time to answer exactly that. How can you as a reader, translate this insight into action?

To do so, you must now turn the lens on yourself. By first decoding how a rapidly evolving global talent pool has an impact on your organization, you can eventually assemble the ingredients for your strategic response. Simply put, in this chapter my goal is to help you prioritize your unique set of talent strategies and improve the returns on your talent investments.

The current state of talent strategy

During the three years it took to research and write this book, I travelled all over the world, speaking, training and interviewing leaders on local or global trends and how they correlated to talent strategy. During dozens of keynotes, in places as diverse as Barcelona, Singapore, Mumbai, London, Manila or Hong Kong, I would often ask the audience of CEOs, business leaders and HR executives to take a few moments and reflect on how they currently go about creating (and executing) a strategic talent agenda.

Here's what I found:

- Most had some form of an annual plan. A kaleidoscope of programmes, projects, processes or solutions, this annual plan primarily targeted a set of current problems, for example reducing employee turnover, increasing the pool of middle managers or improving pockets of low employee engagement. In the same vein, many fondly spoke of the global programmes they were rolling out – important strategic programmes aimed at strengthening leadership skills or top talent development.

- Frequently, as I heard them speak, I would spot an underlying overlap in scope. Their annual people plans included the organization's talent needs on the one hand and the HR department's needs (for example introducing a new talent management process or tool, ramping up flexible working, improving ERP software, redesigning compensation plans) on the other. Indeed, these HR projects do help a company manage its people better but, to use a sporting analogy, a groundsman's goal to prepare a good soccer pitch cannot be mixed up with a coach's strategy to win a soccer game.

- Only a handful of those in my audiences based their agenda on strong trend analysis or illustrated their strategy using data.

When present, analysis was mostly internal, for example involving employee attrition numbers, employee satisfaction scores or hiring statistics.

- I saw lots of disconnected practices. Indeed, many respondents seemed preoccupied with processes built around someone else's best practices. It was almost as if they believed that installing a succession planning system, or a new promotion process or a nine-box assessment, would in itself help resolve burning talent challenges.

- When asked who owned the company talent agenda, the answer I most often got was the head of HR. Creating and executing talent strategy was perceived as the HR department's responsibility, with support and input from business leaders.

One MD had the room in splits by honestly admitting that he couldn't remember the specifics of his talent agenda. All that he could recollect was that it had been presented recently by his HR team, was presented on approximately 40 PowerPoint slides, and currently sat safely locked away in his top drawer. I couldn't suppress a chuckle too, for he had just helped me illustrate my next point, superbly.

Many companies create reams of beautiful PowerPoint presentations in the name of talent strategy, yet struggle to get all leaders singing off the same 'strategy' sheet.

Strategy is worst communicated through complex presentations that invariably gain airtime once or twice a year. On the contrary, to be successful, strategy needs to be simple, rooted in forward-looking analysis, and widely understood. It also needs to be executed deep within the business and visibly championed at the top.

Talent strategy is the same. HR has a role to play, but it cannot be a central one. That job belongs to the CEO.

To truly craft a 'top-drawer' strategic response, I propose three fundamental principles for any talent strategy.

1 **Talent strategy must start with deep diagnosis, and respect for contextual differences.** The starting point of strategy is analysis focused both on external trends and the internal forces helping or hindering business growth. We want to be able to distinguish symptoms from their causes and map opportunities and risks within an overall talent system. Context is important

too. We have seen throughout this book how dramatically talent dynamics differ from country to country. It is sometimes easy to forget that even in the most global of organizations, 90 per cent of talent is local. Hence talent strategy must also be locally relevant.

Let's look at leadership development practices as an example. It is fallacious to assume that a standard three-day leadership development programme is going to address leadership challenges equally in São Paulo or Seattle or Shanghai. It often does the opposite, by distracting us from the subtly different yet equally real set of challenges that leaders in each location face. It isn't surprising in the least then, to hear the recent clamour about demonstrating the ROI (return on investment) on these 'spray and pray' leadership programmes.

What we need instead is leaders in each location who commit to developing the next generation of leaders. Not in the classroom, but on the shop floor.

Given the diversity of talent issues across a global firm it is often impossible for one central strategy to address all needs. While central planning may work in smaller firms operating out of one or two key locations, for large companies spread across the world, every key cluster must have locally anchored strategy. Strategy must also be focused on the 'many' and not just on the 'few'. In other words, strategic efforts must reflect the needs of all employee segments, all key locations and all parts of the business. It isn't prudent to focus investments and efforts on a small subset of the population, for example just top talent, or the top 200.

2 **Talent strategy must be built with a time and investment viewpoint.** We want to be able to address short-term and long-term needs. Hence strategy must ideally have a three–five-year viewpoint. Never just one year. That's because an annual plan can only address short-term needs, in a short-term manner. Similarly, if we are serious about our strategic choices, we must invest time, leadership energy and, importantly, money into them. This is as serious an investment as any a company makes, and hence should be able to deliver quantifiable business value. This brings me to why talent strategy efforts must be the responsibility of business leaders.

3 **Talent strategy must be owned by the CEO.** And by that definition not delegated to the HR function. The HR department has a key role to play during analysis, in supporting execution and as an overall facilitator; but accountability for execution of long-term talent strategy must rest with the business leader. Later in this chapter we will discuss how CEOs can build a broad coalition to drive focus and execution.

Your talent strategy doesn't have to be complex. In fact, I often encourage my clients to express each location's talent strategy on one page. A short focused manifesto is much easier to remember, track and communicate than 20 PowerPoint slides. The process to arrive at this one page manifesto, though, should be rigorous. We want to create a well-researched battle plan to win not just today's but also tomorrow's war for talent.

Step 1 – Diagnosis

'As any doctor will tell you, prescription before diagnosis is gross malpractice.'

Given the global talent landscape in 2020, we have a choice to make. On one hand we can wait and react to cues as they appear, or we can choose to be proactive and, we hope, one step ahead of the competition. I think this choice is an easy one, for as Chapter 5's sections on innovation showed us, this is the age of the market maker.

As we brainstorm for options and strategic choices, let's start with the six core questions you must answer.

- How will the future talent landscape affect my business? I hope this book has sparked some thoughts in your mind already. Identify the talent trends that have a direct impact on you.

- How similar or different are the talent challenges in each of our key locations? The global talent pool is getting more and more differentiated; and as we have seen, while some talent trends are global, many more are local, or regional in nature.

- What are our standout strengths? Your current talent stays with you for a reason. Identify the parts of your culture that can be accentuated.

- Where do we need to reinvent current practices? The truth is every company, no matter how successful, is still 'work in progress'. Identify the management practices that could prevent you from retaining or attracting the right people in 2020 and beyond.

- Who are my talent champions and what does our talent coalition look like? You can't do this alone. To be successful, every location needs a critical mass of leaders involved. Who should be involved in this debate?

- How will our business change and how will we grow over the next five years?

An honest debate is a great place to start and will give you ideas on where you need to dig deeper for answers. To help you make the most of a brainstorm or debate though, having the right internal or external data on the table can be very powerful. It can help separate fact from perception and also help manage complex relativities inherent in your business. The more complex your business, the more valuable good diagnosis will prove.

The aim of diagnosis is to arrive at a list of action areas that matter most. These are not just the actions that seem most obvious or most urgent, but priorities that really matter. To identify them you must first expand your ability to see an entire spectrum of competing possibilities, and then use insight to narrow down to a few choices.

I have found there are 11 competing realities that vie for focus and investment within an organization's overall talent context. Some are external to the company, while others are internal. Each is an independent variable, yet collectively they shape our talent priorities. They are:

- the local economic environment;
- the supply of external talent available to your business;
- the quality of external talent available to your business;
- the maturity and market share of your business;
- your market standing as an employer;
- your internal talent demography;

- your current management maturity;
- your flow circumstances;
- your innovation index;
- your growth and change agenda;
- your business strategy.

Put together, these 11 perspectives provide a very competent diagnostic profile of your company's talent needs. Let's understand each one better.

The local economic environment

The best place to start diagnosis is with an 'outside-in' view of your business. Ask yourself: What are our business circumstances and how does this affect my talent choices?

Funnily enough, I didn't learn this from a heavyweight executive, but from a well-weathered sailor. You see, out in the open water, far away from any form of support, successful sailing is all about mastering your circumstances. Sailboat captains spend most of their time reading the wind and the water, before adjusting sheets, sails and rudder for the conditions on offer. Crafting talent strategy is similar. Start by studying the wind and weather surrounding your business. In doing so I would encourage you to consider both a country and industry view.

The country view

How mature are the external circumstances for business? Consider factors such as labour practices, capital market maturity, intellectual property laws, political stability and recent patterns of economic growth. For a single location business, this will be relatively easy. However, if your is a global company, with hundreds of offices, I would recommend evaluating the countries that have 5 per cent or more of your global headcount, or generate over 5 per cent of your global revenues.

The industry view

What is the rate of growth and change in your industry? Is the overall revenue pie of your industry growing, or is it in decline? Similarly, what is the rate of innovation, technological obsolesce or regulation change?

To help us capture your diagnosis I propose we use a simple continuum, as shown in Figure 6.1.

FIGURE 6.1   Market opportunity

Developed	1	2	3	4	5	6	7	8	9	10	Emerging

Using this continuum helps us distinguish one location from another and accurately reflect the relative business circumstances.

CASE STUDY

My clients in Japan almost always pick a low number, reflecting the maturity of competition, regulation and technology in what probably is the world's most developed market. Contrast this with China, Nigeria or Vietnam – markets that offer huge upsides for growth, but at significant operational risk. Here the consensus number on the market opportunity continuum could be 9 or even 10.

Similarly, it is easy to classify your industry using the same continuum.

CASE STUDY

The energy business affords us a good industry example. Most people would say that petroleum refining is a mature and well-developed business. Competition is high, technology is well developed and margins are similar across a number of industry players. On the other hand, green technology firms represent a chaotic, risky and still untested industry, where potential is immense but the rules of businesses are still emerging.

Where you sit on this continuum depends both on the market and the industry you operate in. Sometimes we see developed industries embedded within emerging markets and vice versa.

CASE STUDY

Despite operating in an emerging country and a relatively young industry, many outsourcing companies I surveyed in India chose a low number, signifying how vast and competitive the Indian outsourcing business is at the moment.

Market opportunity has a material impact on talent strategy. Growing world-class talent in emerging markets requires greater focus and investment than in more stable environments. The risks are different too, with retention of key talent being one of them.

The supply of external talent available to your business

Continuing to work outside-in, while crafting strategy you need to be mindful of the availability of talent. How much high-quality talent can you find in this location? In this case the continuum looks like Figure 6.2.

FIGURE 6.2   Market talent pipeline

Abundant	1	2	3	4	5	6	7	8	9	10	Scarce

This is where the analysis of macro talent trends comes in very handy. Education, migration, ageing populations and generational shifts all affect the composition of available talent, as does the impact of government policy.

Consider also your leadership mix through all levels of your company – particularly the number of women in senior roles and a healthy pipeline of local leaders. Both demographics are impossible to ignore today.

Women represent the fastest growing segment on college campuses today. Companies who don't have an equitable mix of women leaders are rightly under pressure from everyone – shareholders, analysts and even governments.

Creating a strong cohort of local leaders is another area of critical focus, as is finding a balance between local and expatriate leadership talent. While expatriation as a means of sourcing talent has grown rapidly in recent years, and proves an effective short-term option, many companies have started realizing how risky an over-reliance on expatriates can be in the medium to long term. For one, it is a very expensive strategy. For another, every global relocation carries an enhanced risk of executive failure. Each market context being so different, a high potential leader in one could easily become mediocre in another. Finally, as some companies have painfully discovered, overcoming a lack of local talent by importing expatriates can further exacerbate the problem in developing local leaders. Over time, talented locals may perceive a glass ceiling and leave.

If you must redial some of your key demographics, you must start by scoping out availability of talent in the external market. Even if talent is scarce, increasing economic volatility can present unique opportunities to smart and prepared businesses. For example, during the 2009 slump, smart companies were able to handpick graduates off campus and bring in precious middle-management talent while others were letting them go. Even in markets such as China, Vietnam, South Africa or Russia where management talent is scarce, these opportunities do present themselves with surprising regularity, if we keep an eye out for them.

As strategists our goals are to identify the talent trends that work to our advantage, and arrive at our own 'buy and build' equation for the future. And this differs from one location to another.

CASE STUDY

The healthcare business in Europe faces an acute shortage of nurses today to meet the demands of its ageing population. In other locations, such as the Philippines, an abundance of nursing schools graduate over 40,000 nurses a year.

Now if you were running a chain of hospitals growing throughout the world, how would you respond to this supply imbalance?

In every market experiencing a scarcity of trained talent, there could still be positive supply trends. One example is the supply of engineering graduates in China. As we saw in Chapter 4, since the early 1990s China has made impressive investments in tertiary technical education. We are now beginning to see the fruits of this investment through a growing abundance of talent, particularly in engineering industries. An article by Charles Duhigg and Keith Bradsher entitled 'How the U.S. Lost Out on iPhone Work', published in the *New York Times* on 21 January 2012, looked at reasons why Apple chose to manufacture its iPhone in China rather than the United States: 'Apple's executives had estimated that it needed about 8,700 industrial engineers for the iPhone project. The company's analysts had forecast that it would take as long as nine months to find that many engineers in the United States. In China, it took 15 days.'

What are your talent supply risks or opportunities? Study the market to identify where your talent comes from and what your 'buy or build' equation looks like.

The quality of external talent available to your business

Just the volume isn't enough. The quality of skills people possess matter too. Consider a prominent location for your company today, and ask yourself how easy it is to find 'skilled and ready-now' talent in this location. If the answer is it's not easy, then you need a clear strategy either to import skilled labour or set up the infrastructure to develop capabilities within. This is a fundamental question, as it instructs the architecture and investments of your hiring and training efforts.

Companies that investigate and establish this trend early are at a significant advantage, because they can capture space further upstream before the competition. Let's go back to China for a moment. With better infrastructure connecting central China to its ports, many global businesses are moving further inland to cities where labour and land are considerably cheaper.

CASE STUDY

In 2003, when Intel chose Chengdu for its second plant in China, it didn't do so without assessing the talent pipeline. With a definite plan to hire thousands of local graduates, Intel's trainers visited technical schools in the area to assess curricula and eventually partnered with local institutions to introduce courses on semiconductor physics and factory processes to students (*InTech*, 2006).

I called this the proficiency continuum, and it looks something like Figure 6.3.

FIGURE 6.3   Pipeline proficiency

Ready skills	1	2	3	4	5	6	7	8	9	10	Ready potential

Where you sit on this continuum has a deep bearing on your talent strategy, but be careful to assess your key hiring locations independently. The case study below shows why.

CASE STUDY

When a major investment bank was looking to grow its fixed income trading business in Asia, it found a singular strategy just wouldn't work in the region. While it was relatively easy to find highly qualified candidates of international calibre in Hong Kong, Mumbai and Singapore, in other locations like Jakarta, Shanghai or Manila, the experience was exactly the opposite – hiring managers could find precious few. The Indonesian business eventually chose to hire fresh finance graduates who were put through a two-year rotational programme before being allowed to transact independently. In China, talent had to be hired from Singapore and Hong Kong, a process that took longer and delayed revenue growth plans. The Singapore office on the other hand, already had its new traders handling transactions by the end of their second week.

By analysing the quality of talent available, a company can also start mapping how much time it takes to make a new hire independently productive. I call this the 'time to proficiency' metric and the example above clearly demonstrates how much this number can vary.

For companies or locations at the lower end of the continuum (with ratings 1–3), time to proficiency could be a matter of weeks or a few months. For roles on the other end of this spectrum (with ratings 7–10) where companies may need to hire purely for potential and train for skill, the time to proficiency could be several months or even years.

The maturity and market share of your business

Jack Welch had a simple principle on market share, which he ensured that all business heads at GE understood: 'If you aren't number one or number two in your industry, we will shut down your business or divest it.' As draconian as this may seem, he had a point. Business isn't like middle-distance running where the strongest hang back and the weakest set the pace. In the cold, hard commercial world, it's easier to get customers, source funds, build partnerships and even find talent if you are number one.

In short, leaders have a better chance of winning. Yet in global business, even if a company is an outright market leader in its industry, it doesn't necessarily mean it is number one in every market or product it retails. Procter & Gamble (P&G) is a good example.

CASE STUDY   P&G

Throughout this book we have seen P&G's exemplary practices in product innovation or leadership development come up for praise. But being the world's number one personal and home products company, doesn't mean it leads its rivals in all products or all geographies. While P&G is a clear market leader in the United States and the Philippines, it trails local competitors significantly in France and China. In other countries, for example India, it has been a late entrant compared to arch rival Unilever, and had to grow its business from an embryonic start in 1989, almost half a century after Unilever entered the country. On the ground, in countries where it trails the leaders, this does influence P&G's attractiveness as an employer.

Review where you sit on the market share continuum (Figure 6.4). Your score may differ for each of your key markets. Where are you a market leader? Where are you still subscale or outside the top five in your industry?

FIGURE 6.4 Market share

Industry leader	1	2	3	4	5	6	7	8	9	10	Embryonic

This has a significant impact on our talent strategy. In countries where your market share is still small, or you are trailing the dominant player or players, you will need to invest in differentiating yourself as an employer. You may even need to spend more in building your employment brand and attracting the right talent to join. The starting point for attraction (and retention), as we saw in Chapter 5, is building a solid and honest employee value proposition (EVP). As Shackleton showed us a century ago, this must be deeply anchored in reality, yet offer a sense of purpose.

Your market standing as an employer

Conjoined to where you currently stand in your industry, also consider how attractive an employer you are. One way of doing this is looking at where you hire from and who hires from you. The continuum shown in Figure 6.5 can help clarify your relative position.

FIGURE 6.5 Talent attraction

Employer of choice	1	2	3	4	5	6	7	8	9	10	Challenging

If you picked a low number, it should be because you find it easy to attract talent from your competitors, for similar jobs without paying a premium. Talent wants to join you, and if you hire from college campuses, then you should already be a highly coveted employer among the student body.

If on the other hand you picked a high number, it would probably be because significant quantities of your talent leave to join your competitors. You may find retaining high performers is difficult and you often come away from campus-hiring exercises without a fair haul of quality candidates.

Here's the problem. Very often companies who are perceived as employers of choice aren't necessarily doing spectacular things for their employees, at least not more than the organizations they compete with for talent. But because their brand is better known, they are bigger in size, they have headquarters in a particular location, or a hundred other factors, their grass just seems greener. Perceptions can be brutal, and often companies who find themselves in a challenging spot can justifiably feel victimized. All is not lost though, and as long as you offer a quality employment experience perceptions can be changed, as the example below shows.

CASE STUDY

India has some of the most aggressive companies in the world, and many of them – after decades of impressive local growth – are dreaming of going global. India's largest telecom company, Bharti, is growing rapidly across Africa; Indian company JK Tyre recently bought and turned around Latin America's largest tyre maker Tornel; the Tata group, one of India's oldest and most respected business houses, has made a slew of international acquisitions including marque brands such as Tetley, Jaguar, Land Rover and Corus. What's more, the Tata group's hotel arm now runs the iconic Pierre on New York's 5th Avenue.

All this hasn't gone unnoticed. After years of dreaming of multinational careers, the majority of Indian talent now clearly prefers working for an Indian company. A 2010 survey (Aon Hewitt and JobStreet, 2011) showed that in India local employers were preferred over those from the United States, the United Kingdom, Japan or Germany. However, when these same Indian companies try and hire overseas, they plainly hit a wall. Respondents in places such as Singapore, Malaysia, Philippines and Indonesia rate Indian companies as their least preferred employers, well below Western multinationals and even lower than other Asian employers. If Indian companies are to make a successful global transition, changing this perception will be a key area of focus and investment.

Your internal talent demography

In the section on microeconomics we covered how critical corporate culture is to employees' success. And nowhere is this truer than with fresh talent. If the EVP is a reflection of reality, new joiners have a better chance of success. However, to be successful, every employee still needs to go through what I call the five stages of assimilation – subscribe, discover, understand, create equity, distribute equity (see Chapter 5).

Every new employee starts out highly dependent on others, for information, introductions, job assistance, emotional support and, most importantly, affirmative encouragement. If this exists, the journey from dependence to independence is an easy one. In time, uncertainty melts away and is replaced with calm confidence. Independence is good. It creates comfort, and feeds performance aspirations; but it won't make a company great. The best organizations help take employees beyond independence to a stage of interdependence, where they help each other succeed and where they play as a team. Figure 6.6 reminds us of the five steps that help an employee get there.

FIGURE 6.6   The five stages of assimilation

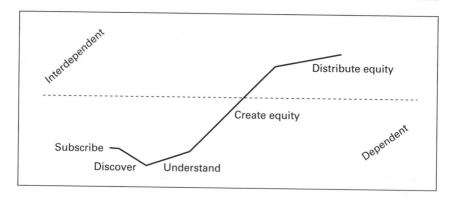

This journey across the five steps takes time and can typically stretch from a few months to a few years. It takes time to learn, build alliances, test ideas and eventually experience continued success. Further, in the subscribe, discover and understanding stages, the employee is largely dependent on others in the organization for information, investments in learning, opportunities to meet or work with new people, and most of all regular coaching and feedback. This eventually creates enough cultural comfort and confidence in an employee to test new ideas and approaches and with it the journey to creating and eventually distributing equity (supporting others' success) begins. Further, in an interdependent organization, the cycle perpetuates itself automatically. Older employees take pride in supporting new employees' transition from dependence to interdependence, by sharing knowledge, coaching or underwriting early success.

Why time in residence is important

Great organizations have a strong and deliberate process to support employees through their phase of dependence. New employees need significantly more investment, time and structured development in the first years at a company, and remain deeply grateful for the early support they receive.

Spend a few moments looking at the composition of your existing workforce. How many have had less than a year in the company? How many have had less than two years? Are you currently doing enough for them?

CASE STUDY

Consider this example of a globally diversified company that has grown its international division aggressively over the last five years. Figure 6.7 shows the tenure distribution at the company's corporate headquarters, Figure 6.8 shows the regional office, and Figure 6.9 illustrates a relatively young country operation.

FIGURE 6.7

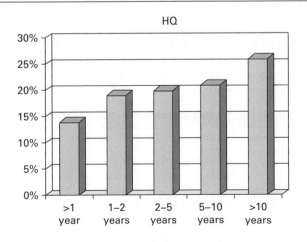

FIGURE 6.8

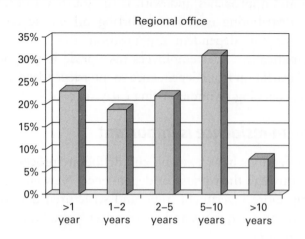

FIGURE 6.9

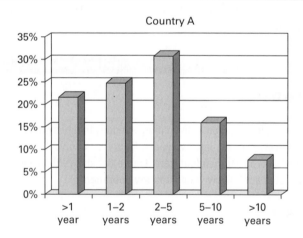

It is clear that in all three locations, a fair percentage of employees have had less than two years in the company (33 per cent of employees at HQ, 42 per cent at the regional office and 47 per cent in country A). This stands to reason, given the company's steep recent growth.

Given the five stages of assimilation, the first two years are critical to move an employee from a position of dependence to a position of secure interdependence. Hence companies must focus on enhancing support during this period. Success within the first 24 months helps an employee climb the equity curve. These investments in effective 'onboarding', building networks and enhancing culture pay rich dividend in the long run.

In the case study company's example, the relatively few employees with over 10 years' experience in both the region and country could also potentially mean a paucity of culture and success mentors, ie those who are already interdependent and could help distribute equity to those who aren't. I would prioritize these locations for investments in early onboarding and culture building.

Use the continuum shown in Figure 6.10 to assess where your organization sits on employee vintage.

FIGURE 6.10   Employee vintage

Tenured	1	2	3	4	5	6	7	8	9	10	Young

If you manage multiple locations, analyse the age distribution in each. If the population is large, break it down by layers within the hierarchy, so you can compare peers. Then look at the ratio of employees on the dependent curve against those who support them. To gain a deeper understanding, study the demographic beyond just tenure. How do generations differ in this location? What is the gender split?

Ask yourself: How can we welcome our newer employees better? How can we amplify their voices, and learn more about them? And how can we better support their success?

Your current management maturity

When I was starting out as an executive coach, a mentor of mine told me: 'Organizations rise and fall on the strength of 50 people. Find out who they are and help them play their best game'.

Years later, I can certify these words rang true for every company I have helped, irrespective of size, location or industry. If we can get the people who matter most to lead effectively, over 90 per cent of the leadership issues further downstream disappear automatically.

That's because leadership culture isn't built through training programmes and competency models, it is built through values and behaviour. The trick is to find out quickly who the key influencers are, study their technique, and help them understand how they as individuals build or destroy the company's leadership culture.

Finding them is the key though. In Western organizations, I start with the organization chart and then sit through a few meetings. Invariably, the influencers sit nearer to the top of the pyramid and occupy critical seats at the table. In a meeting, they are the ones whose opinion is always sought, and when they speak, everyone perks up to listen.

In other cultures, finding the culture carriers is slightly trickier, it requires much more observation and maybe even an insider's viewpoint. In a lot of Chinese firms, for example, the organization chart is the worst place to start. Many key influencers and culture carriers don't figure in the chart at all. They sit on the margins, driving business decisions in the background. Other factors may matter more than title or responsibility, such as external affiliations or networks. In many Indian firms, it isn't uncommon to find a lot of friends and family on this list. Relationships matter more than role, as does tenure and trust.

No matter where they sit, in the foreground or background, the way these key culture makers behave and interact is observed by everyone. And it is mirrored.

When diagnosing your company's management culture, look at it from two perspectives. First, look at how strong the culture of leadership is in your senior management group. You may find that some within this group are highly skilled and hence seen as credible role models. Others in the group may be struggling to lead. You may also spot young leaders still learning the ropes or others in decline due to loss of desire or purpose. Second, look at how members of this group work together. Observe their mechanisms. Are they a loose coalition or do they operate as a team? Do they trust each other and play to a common game plan, or is the atmosphere factious and politically charged?

Use the continuum shown in Figure 6.11 to assess where you see the senior management group today.

FIGURE 6.11   Management ability

Developed	1	2	3	4	5	6	7	8	9	10	Inconsistent

If you scored the senior management group close to developed, this is great news and you are at a distinct advantage. If on the other hand you rated your management group at between 6 and 10, helping your senior team succeed will probably prove to be one of your most important strategic priorities.

Your flow circumstances

'*People who learn to control inner experience will be able to determine the quality of their lives, which is as close as any of us can come to being happy.*' MIHALY CSIKSZENTMIHALYI

These words from Csikszentmihalyi (1990) are as true about organizations as they are about people. Flow is all about focus, backed by energy. Organizational flow, as we discussed earlier, is about pursuing clear goals with collective energy. It is a state when all parts of the company, customer facing and support, product A and product B, country C and country D, collaborate with a common aim.

We want an organization that accentuates employees' energy, and can collaborate across boundaries. We don't want independence; we want interdependence – the ability to help each other win.

Ask yourself: How easy it is to manoeuvre across my company? And while doing so, focus on the following five enquiries:

- **How clear is the big picture?** Do all employees buy into the organization's overall goals and strategy, as compared to their own function's or unit's success?

- **How do we create insight?** To begin with, can people easily access information when they need it? Particularly, can they easily access information that may help employees serve their clients better. How strong are the lines of two-way communication? Consider both top–down communication and the quality of dialogue across offices, business units or regions.

- **How do we share talent?** How mobile is the internal workforce? How easy is it for people to seek roles in other parts of the organization? Are they encouraged to do so?

- **How do we collaborate?** How strong is the culture of contribution? Do teams or sub-units compete or contribute to each other's success?

- **How do we manage?** How is the company organized? Is it structured around geographies, along strict lines of business, or is it a matrix? How many bosses do middle managers have? What is the speed of decision making?

Answering these questions will give you a fair idea of where you sit on the continuum shown in Figure 6.12.

FIGURE 6.12   Organization structure

Simple	1	2	3	4	5	6	7	8	9	10	Complex

The more fragmented or intricate your company is, the higher your score should be. Complex organizations need to take more deliberate action to create and sustain organizational flow. They need to invest in building lines of communication, and in breaking down artificial boundaries that restrict information or talent. Collaboration must be fostered and recognized. And finally, managers need to be coached and trained to think beyond structure and facilitate big picture success. Otherwise, structural sophistication, which is required at times to manage complex business, will inevitably crumble into in-efficient bureaucracy.

Your innovation index

Japan has a rich tradition of 'hansei' or self-reflection. It is so woven into Japanese society that children, while at school, are taught to regularly step back and perform hansei – reflect on the learning process, their results and how they can improve. It shouldn't surprise us then that in the latter half of the 20th century, hundreds of Japanese companies used the philosophies of total quality management combined with regular reflection to achieve levels of quality, standardization and innovation other countries could only dream about. Improvement was a daily responsibility, even if there was no problem to fix. This was 20th-century innovation.

In the 21st-century, innovation has proven to be quite different. For one, it has become less about continuous small improvements. It is about quantum leaps. It isn't linear any more, it's exponential.

Perhaps that's why Japanese firms, in spite of enjoying the best expertise, resources and brand identity, have struggled to lead in recent times. Leadership isn't about possessing the best technology. It's about possessing the perspective for technological convergence. We see that 400 years after the Medici, their legacy of interdisciplinary innovation is on a comeback.

As we have seen throughout this book, being innovative isn't really a choice any more. It's a subsistence need. And leaders in all kinds of industries are beginning to obsess about it.

Use the continuum shown in Figure 6.13 to map how innovation is viewed in your organization.

FIGURE 6.13   Innovation index

Inert	1	2	3	4	5	6	7	8	9	10	Unrelenting

The best place to start is by looking at the industry you are in. How critical is constant innovation to your competitive success? If you belong to a business that innovates to make its own products redundant, for example the consumer electronics business or e-commerce business, pick a high number. If, on the other hand, most of your innovation originates from a focus on incremental improvement (eg Six Sigma), you reside somewhere in the middle. A low number denotes that your products, technology and customer model hasn't changed materially for at least five years.

If you scored 6 and above, you have a lot to gain by significantly enhancing flow, or raising levels of cerebral engagement across your company. Also focus on the three circumstances for innovation we spoke of in Chapter 5, shown again here in Figure 6.14.

FIGURE 6.14   Creating organizational flow

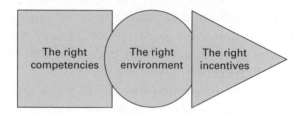

When you create the right environment to brainstorm and collaborate, invest in creative competence and recognize people's ideas, it's easy for innovation to thrive. That's why it is difficult to ignore as a key element of people strategy. Remember, most people are inherently creative and keen to contribute. What they long for though, is a genuine invitation.

Your growth and change agenda

While change is just one of the 11 variables that help delineate an organization's investment priorities, in today's world I would give it a place in the top three. That's because a refusal to change can be brutal, as General Motors discovered.

CASE STUDY

In 2000, General Motors (GM) was the largest company in the world (ranked number 1 in the 2000 Fortune 500). By 2009 it was bankrupt. If there is one overriding factor that took GM straight from number 1 to Chapter 11 within a decade, it was the organization's refusal to read the signs and change. And the signs had been around for years.

For years, Toyota's US operation had been a living example of lean manufacturing and efficient inventory management – right in GM's backyard. Yet this had little impact on GM's executives. GM also let quality slip, right when everyone else – the Japanese, Europeans and Koreans – were in fact investing heavily in raising quality. GM badly misread the shift in US demand to more fuel-efficient vehicles bought on by high gasoline prices. It was as if the oil shocks of the 1970s, 1980s and 1990s had taught them nothing about volatility risks. Many may say the final straw that broke the proverbial camel's back was the global financial crisis. I don't necessarily agree. Immediately before the crisis, during the economic boom, GM raked up over US $50 billion in losses (between 2005 and 2007 alone).

And then the crisis hit. In 2008 alone GM lost US $42 billion.

GM eventually got bailed out by the US government, and may just turn around. Yet for every GM or Kodak that resists change, there is a Nintendo, IBM, or Nokia that embraces it. These companies showed us that changing your DNA isn't easy, but it isn't impossible either.

What are your change circumstances? Look at the horizon. What are the changes facing your industry or organization? Use the spectrum shown in Figure 6.15 to represent your reality.

FIGURE 6.15   Change agenda

Tactical	1	2	3	4	5	6	7	8	9	10	Strategic

Strategic changes take place during a transformative phase for the company, for example, during a merger or a significant company-wide restructuring. They are systemic and have an impact on all employees. From an execution perspective, strategic changes are debated, signed off and watched closely by the board. They are led by the CEO, and could roll out over multiple years.

Tactical changes, on the other hand, represent the day-to-day projects and improvements needed to keep a business moving forward. Often they are localized or have an impact on a subset of the organization. A good example could be a significant software upgrade or introduction of new manufacturing technology. They may transform one process or system, but not the company as a whole.

The higher you rated your change agenda, the higher 'change capability' should rank as a talent priority. You should also consider investments in enhancing communication during times of change, investing in managers' ability to lead change efforts or creating forums for employees to process how change affects them.

Your business strategy

The 11th and final variable is probably the easiest, because it should be at your fingertips already. It deals with your company's business roadmap for the future; let's say the next five years. But first, let's demarcate the line between strategy and aspiration.

Every so often, I come across CEOs who, when asked to talk about their strategy, say things like: 'I think we can double our revenues over the next five years' or 'I believe we can be in the top three within our industry.'

That's great! But, how?

Every destination needs a roadmap. So unless you already have this roadmap in front of you, ask yourself or your leadership team the following 10 questions.

10-steps to strategy

- Where do we want to be in five years? (The aspiration)
- What will help get us there? (The game plan)
- What do we need to change? (Our burning platform)
- Where will we need to invest? (The best use of scarce capital)
- What will our portfolio look like? (Product evolution)
- Why will our customers choose us? (Competitive advantages)
- What are our milestones along the way? (Our scorecard)
- What does success look like? (Hard measures).

Once you have answers to these eight questions, take your strategy through two more gateways:

- What are the biggest risks to success? (Scenarios and contingencies)
- Why should someone invest in us today? (The promise).

Yes, returns always come last, and if the answer to question 10 doesn't meet or beat a fair investment return, go back to question 1 and turn the gas up a notch. As leadership teams start answering these questions, they discover just how steep the road ahead of them is, and it becomes possible to find where your company sits on the continuum of business ambition (Figure 6.16).

FIGURE 6.16 Business ambition

Incremental	1	2	3	4	5	6	7	8	9	10	Aggressive

Incremental ambition doesn't mean a lack of ambition. What it does mean is that the company will largely continue with its past strategic choices. This can be a good thing. The map you drew up in years past is still working. No left or right turns are needed.

Aggressive ambitions, on the other hand, will need some decisive leadership. In some cases it may even mean a complete U-turn, like the one IBM made under Louis V Gerstner Jr in the 1990s, selling off low-margin hardware businesses to transform eventually into a software and consulting powerhouse. If you scored a high number, it invariably means your company will be taking some calculated risks and making some smart bets on the future. It also means, if you are going places, you must put a premium on the talent that will get you there.

The 11 continuums reveal your priorities

If taken in isolation, each and every one of the 11 variables is equally important. It is your context that decides which ones matter more to you than others. But to do that you need to look at the 11 continuums together and compare your scores (see Figure 6.17).

Looking at all 11 together will help you illustrate and objectively weigh your competing priorities. In Figure 6.18, the 11 variables are clustered in three distinct points of view. The first three variables together describe your external talent circumstances. Let's call this the market maturity view.

The next four focus on your organization's internal dynamics. Let's call this cluster the organizational readiness insight. The last four variables describe what lies in your future. This is your organizational aspiration.

All three lenses compete for priority and investment, and as you diagnose your way through them, your talent priorities automatically emerge. You discover the cues for strategy in a proactive and objective manner.

FIGURE 6.17   Strategic talent priorities (1)

		1	2	3	4	5	6	7	8	9	10	
Market opportunity	Developed	1	2	3	4	5	6	7	8	9	10	Emerging
Market talent pipeline	Abundant	1	2	3	4	5	6	7	8	9	10	Scarce
Pipeline proficiency	Ready skills	1	2	3	4	5	6	7	8	9	10	Ready potential
Talent attraction	Employer of choice	1	2	3	4	5	6	7	8	9	10	Challenging
Management ability	Developed	1	2	3	4	5	6	7	8	9	10	Inconsistent
Organization structure	Simple	1	2	3	4	5	6	7	8	9	10	Complex
Employee vintage	Tenured	1	2	3	4	5	6	7	8	9	10	Young
Business ambition	Incremental	1	2	3	4	5	6	7	8	9	10	Aggressive
Market share	Industry leader	1	2	3	4	5	6	7	8	9	10	Embryonic
Innovation index	Inert	1	2	3	4	5	6	7	8	9	10	Unrelenting
Change agenda	Tactical	1	2	3	4	5	6	7	8	9	10	Strategic

FIGURE 6.18   The PeopleLENS

In the absence of diagnosis, we turn reactive and fire-fight the most obvious and urgent issues, often using best practices imported from elsewhere. As I mentioned at the start of this chapter, I have seen companies waste valuable time and money on a list of disconnected projects and talent programmes. They may not hurt you, but they will distract you from what is really needed.

Look at how you scored your organization on the 11 continuums. How many variables received a score of 6 or over? Scores between 6 and 10 denote your most important priority areas. If ignored, they could translate into risks. On the assessment, this is your 'investment zone' (Figure 6.19). The closer you move towards a score of 10, the more critical the need for a strategic play becomes.

Now do this assessment for every critical country or business in your organization, and reflect on the similarities or differences.

FIGURE 6.19   Strategic talent priorities (2)

							Investment zone					
Market maturity	Market opportunity	Developed	1	2	3	4	5	6	7	8	9	10	Emerging
	Market talent pipeline	Abundant	1	2	3	4	5	6	7	8	9	10	Scarce
	Pipeline proficiency	Ready skills	1	2	3	4	5	6	7	8	9	10	Ready potential
Organizational readiness	Talent attraction	Employer of choice	1	2	3	4	5	6	7	8	9	10	Challenging
	Management ability	Developed	1	2	3	4	5	6	7	8	9	10	Inconsistent
	Organization structure	Simple	1	2	3	4	5	6	7	8	9	10	Complex
	Employee vintage	Tenured	1	2	3	4	5	6	7	8	9	10	Young
Organizational aspiration	Business ambition	Incremental	1	2	3	4	5	6	7	8	9	10	Aggressive
	Market share	Industry leader	1	2	3	4	5	6	7	8	9	10	Embryonic
	Innovation index	Inert	1	2	3	4	5	6	7	8	9	10	Unrelenting
	Change agenda	Tactical	1	2	3	4	5	6	7	8	9	10	Strategic

As you do so, ask yourself: How can we make our talent investments relevant to changes in context?

While researching this book, I asked leaders in a variety of global businesses to help me diagnose their talent realities using the 11 continuums. In doing so I was able to collect and study over a 150 profiles, from a range of industries and countries all over the world. The results were astounding. Rarely did two profiles look the same. Even within the same company, each location had an entirely independent set of challenges.

In reality, we aren't fighting a global war for talent: we are fighting several localized conflicts. And each battle is of independent nature. It also reinforces what leaders told us in Chapter 1. The complexity of global business is born from the vast differences in context across the world. I'd like to use four real-life examples to demonstrate what I mean. The first is shown in Figure 6.20.

FIGURE 6.20   Global beverages conglomerate – US country profile

Category	Continuum	Left label	1	2	3	4	5	6	7	8	9	10	Right label
Market maturity	Market opportunity	Developed	**1**	2	3	4	5	6	7	8	9	10	Emerging
	Market talent pipeline	Abundant	1	2	3	**4**	5	6	7	8	9	10	Scarce
	Pipeline proficiency	Ready skills	1	2	3	**4**	5	6	7	8	9	10	Ready potential
Organizational readiness	Talent attraction	Employer of choice	1	**2**	3	4	5	6	7	8	9	10	Challenging
	Management ability	Developed	1	2	3	**4**	5	6	7	8	9	10	Inconsistent
	Organization structure	Simple	1	2	3	4	5	6	**7**	8	9	10	Complex
	Employee vintage	Tenured	1	**2**	3	4	5	6	7	8	9	10	Young
Organizational aspiration	Business ambition	Incremental	1	2	3	4	5	6	7	**8**	9	10	Aggressive
	Market share	Industry leader	1	**2**	3	4	5	6	7	8	9	10	Embryonic
	Innovation index	Inert	1	2	3	4	5	6	7	8	**9**	10	Unrelenting
	Change agenda	Tactical	1	2	3	4	5	6	7	**8**	9	10	Strategic

This company, a well-established global beverages company, is focused on reinventing itself. An employer of choice in the United States, talent acquisition doesn't seem to be the issue at all. Getting a large company to reach out across boundaries and innovate seems to be the burning need. A steep growth ambition requires leaders to invest in platforms that allow cross-functional collaboration. Although management seems developed, another opportunity could be to enhance change leadership capabilities across the firm.

FIGURE 6.21 Regional hospitality company – UAE country profile

Market maturity	Market opportunity	Developed	1	2	3	4	**5**	6	7	8	9	10	Emerging
	Market talent pipeline	Abundant	1	2	3	4	5	6	7	8	**9**	10	Scarce
	Pipeline proficiency	Ready skills	1	2	3	4	5	6	**7**	8	9	10	Ready potential
Organizational readiness	Talent attraction	Employer of choice	1	2	3	4	5	6	**7**	8	9	10	Challenging
	Management ability	Developed	1	2	3	4	5	6	7	8	9	**10**	Inconsistent
	Organization structure	Simple	1	**2**	3	4	5	6	7	8	9	10	Complex
	Employee vintage	Tenured	1	2	3	4	5	6	7	**8**	9	10	Young
Organizational aspiration	Business ambition	Incremental	1	2	3	4	**5**	6	7	8	9	10	Aggressive
	Market share	Industry leader	1	2	3	4	5	6	7	8	**9**	10	Embryonic
	Innovation index	Inert	1	2	**3**	4	5	6	7	8	9	10	Unrelenting
	Change agenda	Tactical	1	**2**	3	4	5	6	7	8	9	10	Strategic

Hospitality is long-term and capital-intensive business that is incredibly dependent on talent for success. Figure 6.21 illustrates a Middle Eastern hospitality company that possesses a fresh and competitive physical product but is clearly struggling on talent. Being subscale in market share, it is struggling to attract quality talent and, as a result, has a relatively young and unstable workforce. Its priorities include a significant programme to upgrade management capability, and building a stronger employment brand to attract talent from more established players. A good EVP can be of great help in doing this. Enhancing the 'early success guarantee' would also help. This could include improving the new employee's experience or investing in inducting and training new employees.

Figures 6.22 and 6.23 are illustrations from the same company, and in fact represent neighbouring business operations. Although Hong Kong belongs to China, it is administered as a special economic region and has circumstances for business that are far removed from those in the parent country. Both the profiles here represent the same business and the same products, yet the priorities are entirely different.

FIGURE 6.22   Global Financial Services Firm – Hong Kong Country Profile

		Left	Scale	Right
Market maturity	Market opportunity	Developed	1 **2** 3 4 5 6 7 8 9 10	Emerging
	Market talent pipeline	Abundant	1 2 3 4 5 6 7 8 **9** 10	Scarce
	Pipeline proficiency	Ready skills	1 2 3 4 **5** 6 7 8 9 10	Ready potential
Organizational readiness	Talent attraction	Employer of choice	1 2 3 **4** 5 6 7 8 9 10	Challenging
	Management ability	Developed	1 2 3 **4** 5 6 7 8 9 10	Inconsistent
	Organization structure	Simple	1 2 3 4 5 6 7 8 **9** 10	Complex
	Employee vintage	Tenured	1 2 3 4 5 6 **7** 8 9 10	Young
Organizational aspiration	Business ambition	Incremental	1 2 3 4 5 6 7 **8** 9 10	Aggressive
	Market share	Industry leader	1 2 **3** 4 5 6 7 8 9 10	Embryonic
	Innovation index	Inert	1 2 3 4 5 6 **7** 8 9 10	Unrelenting
	Change agenda	Tactical	1 2 3 4 5 6 7 **8** 9 10	Strategic

FIGURE 6.23   Global Financial Service Firm
– China country profile

Market maturity	Market opportunity	Developed	1	2	3	4	5	6	7	8	**9**	10	Emerging
	Market talent pipeline	Abundant	1	2	3	4	5	6	7	8	**9**	10	Scarce
	Pipeline proficiency	Ready skills	1	2	**3**	4	5	6	7	8	9	10	Ready potential
Organizational readiness	Talent attraction	Employer of choice	1	2	3	4	5	6	7	**8**	9	10	Challenging
	Management ability	Developed	1	2	3	4	5	6	7	**8**	9	10	Inconsistent
	Organization structure	Simple	1	2	3	4	5	6	7	**8**	9	10	Complex
	Employee vintage	Tenured	1	2	3	4	5	6	7	**8**	9	10	Young
Organizational aspiration	Business ambition	Incremental	1	2	3	4	5	6	**7**	8	9	10	Aggressive
	Market share	Industry leader	1	2	3	4	5	6	7	**8**	9	10	Embryonic
	Innovation index	Inert	1	2	3	**4**	5	6	7	8	9	10	Unrelenting
	Change agenda	Tactical	1	2	3	**4**	5	6	7	8	9	10	Strategic

In China, the business needs investment in developing a robust talent pipeline. Being a young operation focused on retailing existing products, there isn't significant need for change or innovation support. Leaders are saying: 'We know what we need to do, now let's build a team that can get it done.'

On the other hand, the Hong Kong office represents a more mature operation in a mature market. Here, reducing organizational complexity, firing up product innovation and finding next-generation talent to drive growth seems to be the focus area. Furthermore this franchise has been struggling to find and keep talent (reflected in the high scores in both tenure and talent pipeline). Using the 11 variables we can see quite clearly how in this example Hong Kong's strategic priorities are materially different from China's.

Step 2 – Invest in strategic priorities

A robust diagnosis process should have left you with a heightened sense of the priorities across your company. You should now know what sits in your investment zone and would generate the best 'value for effort'. What's more, you should have a clear appreciation of how one location, country or line of business differs from another.

The next step is to craft the solutions and initiatives that will form the backbone of your talent strategy. There are four interests we must consider within this overall strategy:

- **The needs of the individual.** Initiatives aimed at helping people do their job better. These investments bring about improvements in personal capability and represent immediate investments needed in talent acquisition or development.

- **The needs of the group.** From these you can devise solutions that facilitate better interpersonal work or build a positive culture in the organization. These are your organization development investments.

- **Short-term needs.** These are outcomes that must be achieved within the next 6–12 months. These help achieve immediate success.

- **Long-term needs.** These are focus areas for future success. Ranging from two to five years hence, these are outcomes that are still on the horizon but need to be invested in today.

The simple planning matrix shown in Figure 6.24 helps us manage this polarity of time and focus. I call it the PITA model.

The PITA approach helps you clarify the exact recipe of initiatives that make up your talent strategy. When we compare this with the 'annual plan' approach we saw many companies using earlier, the benefits of PITA become clear. In reality annual planning cycles doom you to short-term fixes for long-term problems. The annual plan may also miss the distinction between personal needs and group needs. This leads to some fairly common mistakes.

FIGURE 6.24   PeopleLENS strategy – using the PITA method

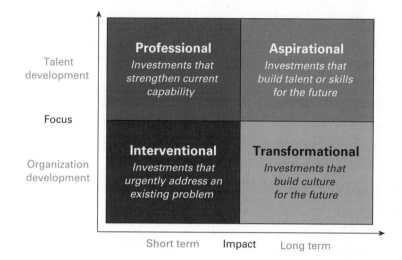

One example of an often misused solution is the leadership development programme. Many companies fail to distinguish between **leader development** (making individuals into better leaders by improving skills such as strategic planning, delegation, change management or a number of other capabilities involved in leading people) and **leadership development** (strengthen an existing leadership team or overall leadership culture by improving alignment between members, improving consistency of message, resolving conflict or eliminating debilitating politics).

Leader development and leadership development are totally different things, and when our strategy does not acknowledge the difference between individual versus group needs, we may end up addressing a problem with an entirely wrong solution.

The PITA approach helps distinguish our needs and eventually balance our strategic agenda. Each quadrant represents a specific type of talent-strategy solution, and the exact recipe of solutions we pick is based wholly on the outcomes of diagnosis. But first let's understand each quadrant.

Professional investments

Professional imperatives help ensure that an organization's workforce stays current and competent. These are investments made in today's performance.

Common examples include:

- investments in attracting and hiring the right talent into open roles;
- assessments (including job assessments, 360-degree surveys and psychometric assessments);
- onboarding and transition support for employees who join;
- training programmes aimed at skilling a workforce for their current job;
- on-the-job learning;
- skills development programmes for managers and leaders;
- executive coaching;
- formal (or informal) performance feedback and coaching;
- conference attendance and trade body memberships;
- communities of practice and other forms of distributed learning.

Aspirational investments

Aspirational investments help prepare an organization's workforce for the future, either by developing people for future roles or by introducing new capabilities. These are investments made in tomorrow's needs. A few examples are:

- campus recruitment programmes;
- internships (including mid-career and returnship) programmes;
- assessment and development centres;
- job rotation arrangements;
- short-term or long-term developmental assignments;
- HiPo (high potential) programmes for identified talent;
- developmental projects;

- external education sponsorships;
- mentoring and job shadowing arrangements;
- business turnaround experiences.

Interventional investments

Interventions focus on fixing a problem or addressing an immediate collective need. They tend to be short, sharp projects with a well-defined outcome, supported by distinct sponsors, with a defined budget and audience. Examples include:

- teambuilding programmes;
- assimilation investments (to support new leaders or new teams);
- T-group and cross-cultural sensitivity programmes;
- quality circles or Six Sigma projects;
- team coaching;
- change management projects;
- investments in cross-functional collaboration;
- investments in leadership team development.

Transformational investments

Transformations are much more long term and focus on the culture an organization wants to build in the future. They help the organization manage its evolution (think of the transformations IBM, Nokia or Nintendo made in the past few decades). Transformational investments are critically important when your company has aggressive growth plans, or is in the midst of significant change such as a merger or acquisition. They are also critical for businesses that operate in immature markets. Common transformational strategies include:

- culture building initiatives;
- visioning workshops;
- business turnaround projects;
- cultural assimilation following mergers or acquisitions;
- immersion programmes for new leaders or new locations;

- industry task forces;
- internal social media development;
- investments in strengthening leader-led 'communicable behaviour' such as role modelling or story telling.

If all you had was US $100, how would you spend it?

Every organization has a distinct PITA recipe. And a large diversified business may even have a different recipe for each key location.

Ask yourself: If I had only US $100 dollars (or for that matter 100 units of energy) to invest, where would I put it? The answer lies in diagnosis. Go back to your 11 variables. Which ones fell into the investment zone? Overlay that understanding onto the PITA model. What solutions would help you make the best use of your precious dollars?

If you had high scores in pipeline proficiency, management ability, employee vintage or innovation, check if there are professional investment plays that would help you. If your market talent pipeline is weak, or you had high priorities on talent attraction or have high business ambitions, aspirational investments may help you grow your talent in line with business growth. For complex organization structures, inconsistent management or an aggressive change agenda, think of the interventions that may help you and, finally, if you operate in an underdeveloped market, are targeting aggressive growth or are currently subscale in revenue, you will need to fund your long-term transformational agenda to steer your organization in the right direction.

At the end, the quality of your strategy will depend directly on the quality of debate in your leadership team. It is this debate that will help your organization arrive at the best set of solutions. If this debate is rich, you may at the end arrive at a clear set of strategic plays backed by a clear investment formula that looks something like Figure 6.25.

Whether your budget is a US $100 or US $100 million, the process is the same. In large companies you may need a talent strategy for each major pocket of operation. Remember the first principle of strategy we began this chapter with: talent strategy must start with deep diagnosis and respect contextual differences. If the context differs, the outcomes of diagnosis will too. Eventually, we want to

FIGURE 6.25   Company ABC – 10-point talent strategy for 2014 (budget US $100)

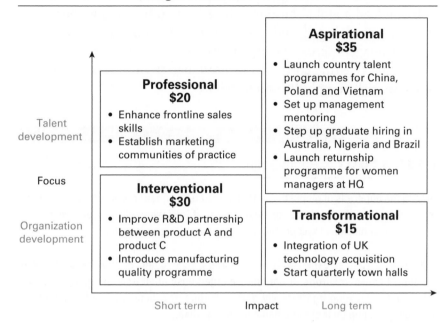

bridge the gap between your needs and your investments. Using the PITA method ensures that the connection between your priorities and actions are clear.

Note: The talent economics toolkit at the end of this book includes a set of PeopleLENS strategy templates for your personal use.

Step 3 – Ownership and focus

'Wisdom is knowing what to do next, skill is knowing how to do it, and virtue is doing it.' DAVID STARR JORDAN

Strategy is a map, not a journey. The journey lies in effective execution of strategic imperatives. And this journey cannot be delegated. It cannot be travelled by proxy. In large organizations this means leaders all across the organization must participate both in formulation and execution of talent strategy. Doing so won't just help them understand their talent needs better; it will help develop them as leaders too.

If you lead a global business, there is merit in making your talent strategy broad based and decentralized. We do this by involving senior managers across the organization. Because if we rely solely on one perspective (the corporate or headquarter view) or one function (HR), we risk an uphill climb to failure.

CASE STUDY   Handelsbank

Among the hundreds of global banks that dominate the finance world, there is one that is different. So different that in the last quarter of 2008 when all its peers were in the midst of living hell, this bank posted its best quarterly result in history.

Welcome to Handelsbank. With headquarters in Sweden, Handelsbank is one of the top 20 banks in Europe. It not only emerged unscathed from the global financial crisis, but is growing aggressively across Europe at a time when other banks are struggling to keep their bloated balance sheets afloat.

Handelsbank isn't small, it operates over 700 branches, employs over 10,000 people and regularly delivers a better return on equity to its shareholders than industry benchmarks. Yet it operates differently from most of its peers. For instance, it doesn't pay yearly bonuses. It does incentivize all staff for success, but pays them only on retirement, as reported in an article entitled 'Proof Banks Don't Have to be Run the Gordon Gekko Way', by Ian Birrell, published in The *Evening Standard* on 19 April 2011. This in itself is ingenious, because it forces employees to seek more intrinsic motivation, such as the satisfaction that comes with building long-term customer relationships.

And Handelsbank believes in decentralization. Within the bank, management use what they call the 'church tower principle' (*Economist*, 2009b) to empower local managers, meaning each branch only seeks to do business as far as one can see from the town's church tower. During the height of the financial crisis, members of each branch team were able to react swiftly, because they knew their customers. This is the level of agility required in a volatile business environment. More so, making local leaders take full responsibility for business success commissions them to think like entrepreneurs would.

Create your coalition

Given how important talent is for business success, talent strategy must sit among the responsibilities of the CEO. But this is only the starting point. Talent circumstances differ so much across the world that expecting one central strategy to address all needs is like packing the same set of clothes for trips to Alaska and Bermuda. The CEO needs to drive his or her focus on talent down to local leaders. As we saw in Handelsbank's example above, in today's highly differentiated and risky global theatre of business, there is virtue in decentralization.

Our aim should be to help local leaders diagnose the talent priorities of their country or business unit and craft strategic responses that follow church tower principles. At a country level, we don't need the entire team of leaders involved, but we do need a critical mass involved, representing both front- and back-office functions.

One client I worked with constituted a 'talent council' of five members from within her overall executive team. This talent council worked directly with the CEO and shared ownership for the overall talent agenda. Over time, members rotated on and off the council, but the council itself proved a huge success in driving the local talent agenda to fruition. Looking forward, I believe that making talent strategy locally relevant, by inviting broad-based participation from local leaders, is probably the safest hedge we have to the complexity trap facing many global businesses today.

The role of HR, strategy and other corporate functions

All over the world, Executive surveys are telling us the same thing: talent is a top three challenge for business, and there's a lot more that we should be doing. This book was born in direct response to this. In the 21st century, successful companies will find that talent decisions must be woven into business decisions. Talent strategy cannot be run in the margins any more; just as talent management can no longer be confined to a process. The fact that talent strategy sits squarely on the business leader's desk does not disenfranchise key functions such as HR. In fact the HR or strategy teams have a key role to play in helping leaders facilitate and aggregate strategy. That should be their role. Expecting more from them effectively takes line leaders off the hook, and places the onus of execution squarely outside the business.

In conclusion, I'd like to go back to the three principles of talent strategy we talked about at the start of this chapter. They are:

- Talent strategy must start with deep diagnosis, and respect for contextual differences.
- Talent strategy must be built with a time and investment viewpoint.
- Talent strategy must be owned by the CEO.

The 11 continuums help us diagnose and compare locations or businesses, and the PITA model helps us build a balanced set of solutions. But all this does is help us arrive at the right car, with the right key. What we now need are leaders willing to start the engine and drive.

Epilogue

'At the very beginning, the world itself was merely an idea.'

Talent economics is much more than a concept. It is a philosophy that has come to suggest the way forward for talent management as a practice. In an age where every company, willingly or unwillingly, must engage and enthuse a global workforce, talent management cannot be reduced to a rigid set of standard operating procedures. Instead we need a little flexibility. We need enthusiastic global leaders willing to participate. We also need empowered local leaders. And our strategic choices must increasingly serve both the needs of the individual and needs of the group. Every trend we have spoken of in this book – some major ones being the developing global system of systems, the major shifts in employee preferences, the fading concept of retirement, or the increasing emphasis on innovation – all have a fundamental impact on your workforce. Logically then, they must also have an equal impact on your management practices. Because at the end, management is nothing but a code. Like good software, it makes the hardware more productive.

Thinkers such as Fayol taught us the science, and leaders such as Shackleton gave us a glimpse into the art, yet management code is less discovery and more invention. In fact, every company invents its own. And hence it can be reinvented, and reinvented again. As it should. Those afraid to invent prefer to copy and become gullible victims of the billion-dollar 'best-practice' industry. Don't get me wrong – best practices are useful reference points, but they must come with a warning label. The more you rely on external intelligence, the less you will value an internal idea. And this is the age of the idea.

Throughout this book, I have preferred to package new and innovative approaches tried by others, as ideas or stories. The only tools I really think you need are those that will help you discover your own context, and through this, your own path forward. **Your code.** The next section gathers a few of these tools together for you to reflect upon. By all means use them, make them your own, and innovate them forward.

If there is one piece of advice I could give you as you go about framing your own talent management code, it would be to throw out the old rulebook, take a wide path around technical jargon and don't be afraid to look in new places for next generation views. Because, as the Medici showed us over 400 years ago, interdisciplinary thinking eventually leads to masterpieces.

The talent economics toolkit

This is a toolkit of resources especially compiled for readers keen to further their research on talent economics, or to apply the concepts and ideas laid out in this book. For more information, first views of new data and regular updates on talent trends, you can also sign up to our monthly talent economics newsletter at **www.PLGAonline.com**

Macro talent economics – data sources

The study of talent economics starts from the analysis of macro trends. We focused on eight core areas in this book, but there is so much data out there, we could dive eight books deep and still not hit bottom. Presented below is a short selection of data sources that might help you get started in mapping talent trends that affect your business.

The global workforce

The best place to start for an aggregate population projection is probably the World Population Projections, which are compiled and offered for free by the Department of Economic and Social Affairs, Population Division of the United Nations. Along with aggregate numbers, you can also find information on migration trends, longevity, replacement fertility and urbanization at **www.un.org/esa/ population/unpop.htm**

FIGURE A.1   Macro talent pyramid

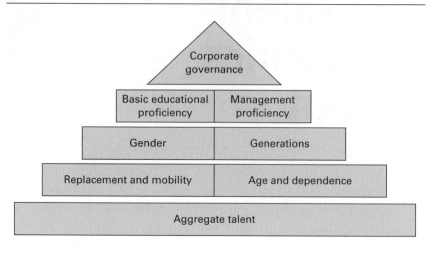

Shifts in the global workforce can be studied through data found in the International Labour Organization (ILO) database: **www.ilo.org/ global/statistics-and-databases/lang–en/index.htm**. This site has a number of country studies, free publications and research reports that you may find useful. For example, you can find the ILO Global Employment Trends 2012 report at **www.ilo.org/wcmsp5/groups/ public/---dgreports/---dcomm/---publ/documents/publication/wcms _171571.pdf**

The Organisation for Economic Co-operation and Development (OECD) statistics website is also a useful resource when studying the 34 member economies. In addition, the site also offers a number of useful publications, such as the OECD fact-book at **www.oecd-ilibrary.org/economics/oecd-factbook_18147364**

Our pipeline of managers, engineers and scientists

This book focused a fair bit on both secondary and tertiary education trends. As talent economists, the educational pipeline is one of the most important indicators of a country's medium-term economic ability. Given that education enrolment and graduation is often tracked at a national level, and each country's formula can differ materially, I recommend you begin from the following universal sources:

- The OECD Programme for International Student Assessment (PISA): **www.pisa.oecd.org**

- Education data from the World Bank/United Nations Educational, Scientific, and Cultural Organization (UNESCO) Institute for Statistics: **www.data.worldbank.org/topic/education**

- The United Nations Development Programme (UNDP) International Human Development Indicators: **www.hdr.undp.org/en/statistics**. This site also has a cool tool to build your own human development index, by comparing countries on a host of human indicators including education.

- To study education trends in individual talent pools, you may need to access country-based sites such as the US-based National Center for Education Statistics (NCES) **www.nces.ed.gov**, or India's All India Council for Technical Education (AICTE) **www.aicte-india.org**, to name a couple.

- You could also access a host of highly credible think-tanks such as Washington DC-based Population Action International **www.populationaction.org**, or IDRC, **www.idrc.ca**, based in Ottawa, Canada. Many universities too have independent research units that track global workforce trends.

- If you would like to review MBA rankings and compare the best management development institutions across countries go to:
  - *Businessweek*: **www.businessweek.com/bschools/rankings/**
  - The *Economist*: **www.economist.com/whichmba**
  - TopMBA: **www.topmba.com/mba-rankings**
  - *The Financial Times*: **http://rankings.ft.com/ businessschoolrankings/global-mba-rankings-2012**

Governance quality

This is a more nascent field of study and hence no one golden standard for governance and sustainability exists. Further, rankings of any sort tend to attract a lot of controversy and criticism. However, given the recent focus on ethical business and sustainable industry practices, mapping standards and trends in governance is an emerging need. For governance, a good place to start is The Worldwide

Governance Indicators (WGI) project: **www.govindicators.org**. In addition, I would also recommend the Environment Performance Indicators (EPI), Yale University and Columbia Business School's global country ranking, which can be found at: **www.epi.yale.edu**

Micro talent economics – applying the concepts

Building your employment value proposition (EVP)

A good starting point is publishing an EVP that is an accurate and existent reflection of your culture. The Executive Board's CLC HR practice has the model shown in Figure A.2, which I particularly like. According to this framework, an EVP emerges from your performance on five core variables – people, work, organization, opportunity and reward. These five variables are in turn made up of 38 factors, as illustrated below.

Here are six steps to creating your organization's employment value proposition:

- **Step 1.** Poll existing employees on what they like about the organization. Even better, ask people who joined your company in the last year about their experiences as new employees. Ask them what they felt the first few months was like – good and bad. If this is the experience you deliver, it serves you well to find people who thrive in this environment.

- **Step 2.** Poll candidates who apply to your organization on what attracted them to the company. Analyse this data to identify trends across employment segments, locations, or business units. Highlight similarities and differences.

- **Step 3.** Study any current employee engagement data you may already have. This could come from quantitative sources such as engagement surveys or qualitative sources like focus groups. Use this data to identify what factors in the current employment climate are your areas of strength.

- **Step 4.** Canvas what your competitors are doing. How do they attract talent? What messages are they using in job adverts, career websites or on campus? How similar or different is this from your own approach and message?

FIGURE A.2 The factors making up the five variables in the CLC model of an organization's employment promise

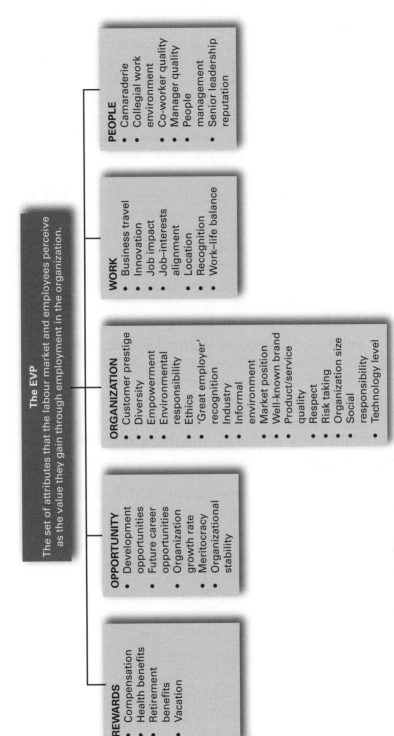

The EVP

The set of attributes that the labour market and employees perceive as the value they gain through employment in the organization.

REWARDS
- Compensation
- Health benefits
- Retirement benefits
- Vacation

OPPORTUNITY
- Development opportunities
- Future career opportunities
- Organization growth rate
- Meritocracy
- Organizational stability

ORGANIZATION
- Customer prestige
- Diversity
- Empowerment
- Environmental responsibility
- Ethics
- 'Great employer' recognition
- Industry
- Informal environment
- Market position
- Well-known brand
- Product/service quality
- Respect
- Risk taking
- Organization size
- Social responsibility
- Technology level

WORK
- Business travel
- Innovation
- Job impact
- Job–interests alignment
- Location
- Recognition
- Work–life balance

PEOPLE
- Camaraderie
- Collegial work environment
- Co-worker quality
- Manager quality
- People management
- Senior leadership reputation

SOURCE: The Corporate Executive Board, CLC Human Resources

- **Step 5.** Aggregate this understanding and formulate your own messages. Identify your standout differentiators. Articulate a compelling value proposition you are confident can be delivered. Describe the experience. One way to do this is by using examples or illustrations of actual employment experience. Sodexo, for example, lists 10 reasons to come and work at Sodexo. One of them is a commitment to support an employee's time preferences: 'We have a variety of jobs to suit your personal circumstances whether you want to work full-time, part-time, seasonally or school hours only.' This is much more powerful than merely saying: 'We encourage flexible working.' The company also uses real-life examples to demonstrate career development: 'Two members of our executive team have worked their way through the ranks. Our corporate affairs director started his career with Sodexo as a unit manager and our commercial director started life at Sodexo as an area manager.'

- **Step 6.** Test this with an informed audience. This could include your internal recruitment teams, head-hunters who know your company well, recruitment firms you work with and other similar informed yet neutral sources.

Focus on early success – the five stages of assimilation

The five stages of assimilation (Figure A.3) describe a journey from dependence to interdependence.

FIGURE A.3

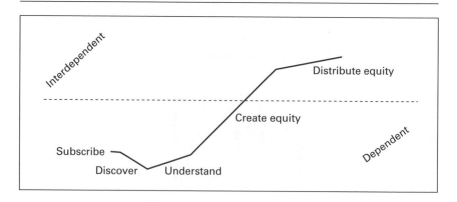

If I were a new employee joining a new company here's how I would experience the stages.

- **Subscribe.** All employment relationships start here. I need to make a commitment and turn up. I would typically be feeling excited; my adrenaline would be pumping, but my enthusiasm would be laced with a shade of trepidation.

- **Discover.** I go through my first few weeks learning on overdrive. Each day seems like a breakthrough. I gather my first experiences and clarify my assumptions. I am starting to discover the culture of this new workplace. I also meet lots of new people and go through strong emotions like validation, inclusion, insight and even some disappointment.

- **Understand.** In a few months, I get into a familiar rhythm. I set some personal rules and start to codify how I can be successful here. The rulebook is now clear and I am able to interpret this organization's culture through every experience. I start forming an early coalition outside my direct team and I am feeling more confident.

- **Create equity.** I am now ready to put my own ideas and strategy into play. There is so much we can improve here. My first successes give me energy to take a bigger risks. By now I have built strong alliances through the firm by finding people I can rely on and call upon for advice. My energy levels are high, as are my hopes for success.

- **Distribute equity.** By now, I see the bigger picture and discover new opportunities to contribute, even if indirectly. I know my thoughts and contribution are valued and I feel less insecure about my personal success. I have gathered a sense of wisdom about how to be successful here and am willing to share this with others.

You could use this framework to help design your induction or mentorship programmes. It could also form an integral part of new manager development, as direct managers are often the greatest enablers of employee success. Finally, analyse and correlate your engagement survey scores to these five stages. What are first year employees saying? How could we help them more?

10 questions that reveal your internal mobility index

We know that 21st-century employees are more mobile, and possess a broader career viewpoint than ever before. In an employment era like the one upon us, this makes internal mobility a virtue. It is also a measure of an organization's health. Losing good people because we were not able to accommodate a 'reasonable' desire for career or geographic mobility is nothing but poor management. To see how geared up your organization is towards internal mobility, ask yourself the following questions:

- Do you have a robust mobility policy; specifying eligibility and process?
- Is it freely shared with all employees?
- Are all open roles advertised internally first?
- Is internal talent preferred when compared to external hires? How is this enforced?
- Do you track and analyse internal mobility?
- Are internal hiring statistics shared with senior managers?
- How do you encourage internal mobility? For example, do you share success stories of internal moves?
- Do employees have access to career counselling? Is this freely advertised and used?
- Are managers encouraged to have an annual career discussion with their direct reports? How many do?
- Are you happy with the following ratio (measured on an annual basis per 100 employees) in your firm? Internal mobility: external hires: resignations.

There is no silver bullet ratio for the last question, though you will instantaneously know which of the three dials is not in tune. To improve this ratio, you must first create the circumstances for mobility:

- Visibly encourage internal mobility.
- Encourage career experimentation.
- Build confidence within employees to share their career aspirations with their managers.
- Offer avenues for career counselling.
- Ensure that all employees have a view of all open roles and set common ground rules for application and hiring.

Especially if you are an industry leader, remember that internal mobility is an imperative, not an option. Poaching from within is a much better outcome than having your competition poach your precious talent.

10 questions to measure and grow cerebral engagement

How does cerebral engagement (Figure A.4) differ from traditional methods of employee engagement?

If you are keen to measure how broad-based employee idea creation and innovation is in your company, ask the following 10 questions (the CE10) to determine cerebral engagement. These questions help you move beyond the traditional emotive and cognitive measures of employee engagement, and identify innovation hotspots and bottlenecks across your company.

- I have ideas on how our company can improve its products or delivery to customers.
- I feel confident sharing and debating these ideas with my manager and other senior colleagues.
- My job directly contributes to my organization's success.

FIGURE A.4   Cerebral engagement

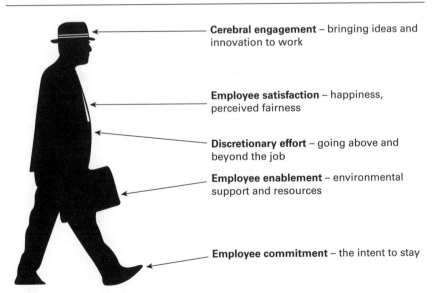

Cerebral engagement – bringing ideas and innovation to work

Employee satisfaction – happiness, perceived fairness

Discretionary effort – going above and beyond the job

Employee enablement – environmental support and resources

Employee commitment – the intent to stay

- My job is intellectually rewarding.
- I have regular opportunities to learn new skills 'on the job'.
- I actively track developments in our industry and what our competitors are doing.
- My goals motivate and challenge me.
- I have the opportunity to collaborate with others on implementing new ideas.
- I don't feel afraid to make a mistake when trying something new.
- I see my manager primarily as my coach.

By polling employees you can begin to map your current circumstances for innovation. Remember this is the clearest indicator of organizational flow in your firm.

21st-century talent strategy

In today's globally connected world, the three principles of 21st-century talent strategy we laid out were:

- Talent strategy must start with deep diagnosis, and respect for contextual differences.
- Talent strategy must be built with a time and investment viewpoint.
- Talent strategy must be owned by the CEO.

Deep diagnosis – connect with your current reality

There are 11 'vectors' that influence your strategic talent choices. As the circumstance for business changes, so must the response. These are:

- the local economic environment;
- the supply of external talent available to your business;
- the quality of external talent available to your business;
- the maturity and market share of your business;
- your market standing as an employer;

- your internal talent demography;
- your current management maturity;
- your flow circumstances;
- your innovation index;
- your growth and change agenda;
- your business strategy.

To get closer to your needs, study each country or line of business within your company operation. Involve local leaders and foster a debate on how their location differs on the three lenses of the PeopleLENS (Figure A.5).

FIGURE A.5 The PeopleLENS

Put together, into a diagnostic assessment, these 11 perspectives help provide a very competent diagnostic profile of your talent priorities.

Assessment date: _____ Assessment done by: _____

FIGURE A.6   Strategic talent priorities (1)

		1	2	3	4	5	6	7	8	9	10	
Market opportunity	Developed	1	2	3	4	5	6	7	8	9	10	Emerging
Market talent pipeline	Abundant	1	2	3	4	5	6	7	8	9	10	Scarce
Pipeline proficiency	Ready skills	1	2	3	4	5	6	7	8	9	10	Ready potential
Talent attraction	Employer of choice	1	2	3	4	5	6	7	8	9	10	Challenging
Management ability	Developed	1	2	3	4	5	6	7	8	9	10	Inconsistent
Organization structure	Simple	1	2	3	4	5	6	7	8	9	10	Complex
Employee vintage	Tenured	1	2	3	4	5	6	7	8	9	10	Young
Business ambition	Incremental	1	2	3	4	5	6	7	8	9	10	Aggressive
Market share	Industry leader	1	2	3	4	5	6	7	8	9	10	Embryonic
Innovation index	Inert	1	2	3	4	5	6	7	8	9	10	Unrelenting
Change agenda	Tactical	1	2	3	4	5	6	7	8	9	10	Strategic

Focus on where you scored 6 or more. This is your investment zone.

FIGURE A.7 Strategic talent priorities (2)

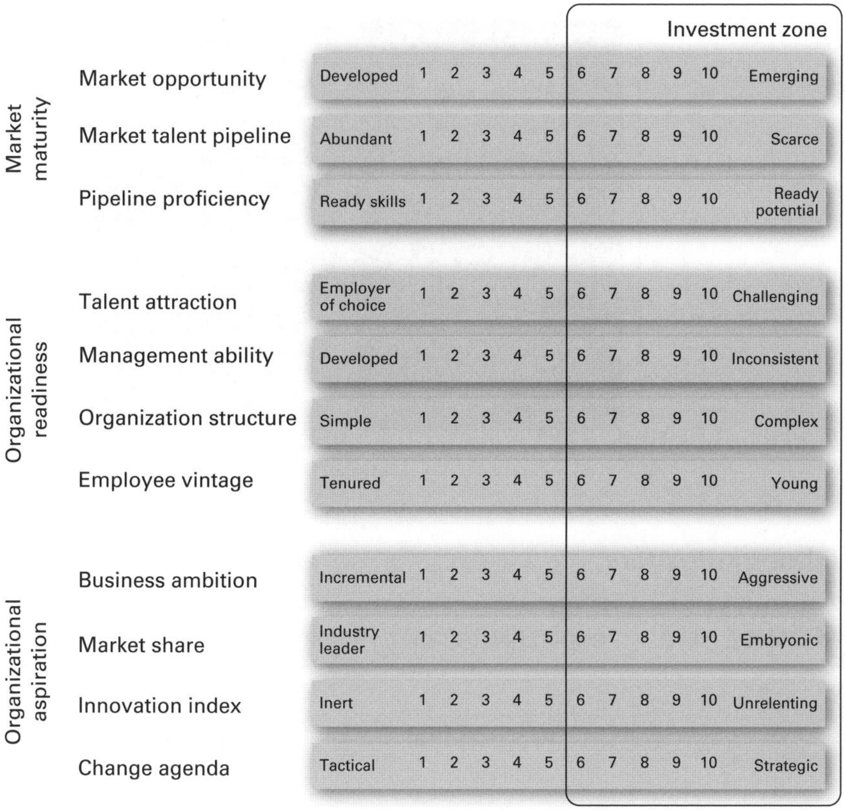

Now translate your priorities into initiatives using the PITA model shown in Figure A.8. I recommend no more than seven or eight strategic priorities at a time. A smaller list is easier to remember and track. This also helps you allocate adequate time and budget for the most important needs. Appoint a business leader to each strategic initiative and give them the tools and support they need to deliver results.

FIGURE A.8   PeopleLENS strategy – using the PITA method

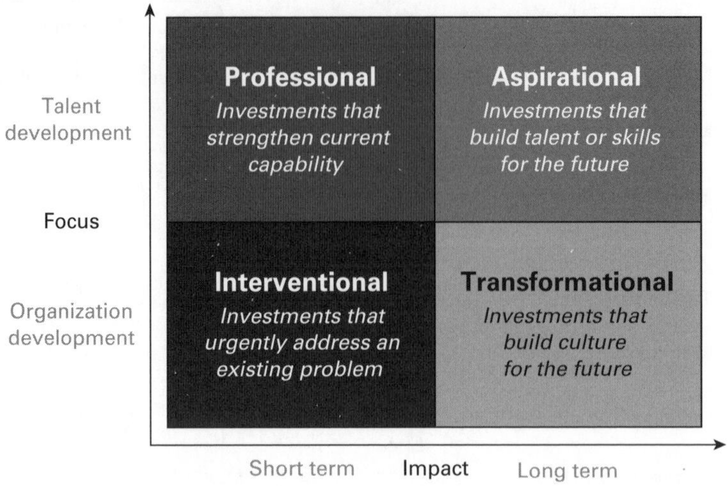

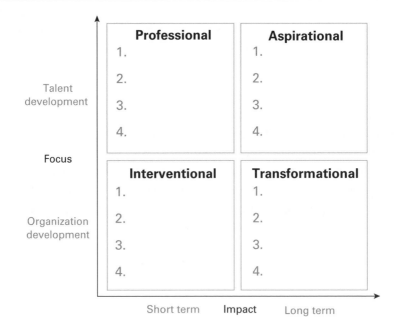

Talent strategy for: _____ Date : _____

FIGURE A.9   PeopleLENS strategy – using the PITA framework

REFERENCES

AICTE (2010) Indian engineering and MBA institutions: growth trends and data [Online, accessed June 2012] www.dreducation.com/2010/12/engineering-mba-trends-data-india.html

Aon Hewitt and JobStreet (2011) Jobseekers' preference survey results, 12 January [Online, accessed June 2012] http://online.wsj.com/public/resources/documents/AonHewittsurvey.pdf

Beinhocker, E D, Farrell D and Zainulbhai, A S (2007) Tracking the growth of India's middle class, *McKinsey Quarterly*, August

Business Times/Centre for Governance, Institutions and Organizations (2011) Governance and transparency index, [Online, accessed June 2012] http://bschool.nus.edu.sg/Portals/0/images/CGFRC/docs/GTIMethodology_11July2011.pdf

Catalyst Research (2010) Women in management in the United States, 1960–present, April [Online, accessed June 2012] www.catalyst.org/publication/207/women-in-management-in-the-united-states-1950-present

CLC Human Resources Executive Board (2009) Engagement research survey, 2009 employment value proposition survey [Online, accessed June 2012] www.performancesolutions.nc.gov/EVP/EmploymentValuePropositionB.pdf

Csikszentmihalyi, M (1990) *Flow, The Psychology of Optimal Experience*, Harper and Row, New York

Economist (2009a) Scrimp and save, 25 June [Online, accessed, June 2012] www.economist.com/node/13887853

Economist (2009b) Back at the branch. More Swedish lessons for the banking industry, *The Economist*, 14 May [Online, accessed June 2012] www.economist.com/node/13606241

Economist (2010) CEO turnover rate [Online, accessed June 2012] www.economist.com/node/16168008, data and graph from Booz and Co research

Engelman, R and Leahy, E (2006) How many children will it take to replace their parents? (Report prepared for the Population Association of America 2006 Annual meeting, Los Angeles, CA, March 30–April 1, 2006), Population Action International, Washington, DC

EOWA (2010) 2010 Census key findings report, Equal Opportunity for Women in the Workplace Agency, see also www.eowa.gov.au

Finette, P (2010) Lesson from Mozilla: How we are learning to foster and grow participation [Online, accessed June 2012] www.scribd.com/doc/31894517/Lessons-From-Mozilla-Open-Innovation-Crowd-Sourcing

Governance Metrics International (2010a) Women on boards: a statistical review by country, sector, and super-sector, March 11 [Online, accessed June 2012] www.gmiratings.com/(bnnl3555sqbsvh551v2jfs55)/hp/Women_on_Boards_-_A_Statistical_Review_from_GMI_-_3_2_09.pdf

Governance Metrics International (2010b) Global corporate governance country rankings [Online, accessed June 2012] http://www2.gmiratings.com/info.php?id=60

Gupta, A K and Wang, H (2009) *Getting China and India Right*, p 206, Jossey-Bass, San Francisco

Hayutin, A (2010) Population age shifts will reshape global workforce, Stanford Center on Longevity

Huston, L and Sakkab, N (2006) P&G's new innovation model, *Harvard Business Review*, March

IBM Corporation (2010) *Capitalising on complexity, insights from the global chief executive officer*, IBM, New York

ILO (2011) Global employment trends, the challenge of a jobs recovery [Online, accessed June 2012] www.ilo.org/global/publications/ilo-bookstore/order-online/books/WCMS_150440/lang–en/index.htm

InTech (2006) Intel creates ecosystem in China, 24 May [Online, accessed June 2012] www.ISA.org

Julius Baer/CLSA (2011) Julius Baer wealth report Asia [Online, accessed June 2012] www.juliusbaer.com/data/docs/download/6324/en/jb-studie-awr-small.pdf

Kaufmann, D, Kraay, A and Mastruzzi, M (2010) The worldwide governance indicators: methodology and analytical issues, September, World Bank Policy Research Working Paper No. 5430

Maddison, A (2007) *Contours of the World Economy, 1–2030 AD: Essays in macro-economic history*, Oxford University Press

McKinsey & Company (2007) Women matter [Online, accessed June 2012] www.mckinsey.com/Features/Women_Matter

McKinsey & Company (2008) Making talent a strategic priority, *McKinsey Quarterly*, January

McKinsey & Company (2010) Global survey results – Five forces reshaping the global economy, McKinsey & Company

Nayar, V (2010) How I did it – A maverick CEO explains how he persuaded his team to leap into the future, *Harvard Business Review*, June

NumberOf.net (2010) Number of MBA graduates in the US per year, based on data from the National Center for Education Statistics (NCES) [Online, accessed June 2012] www.numberof.net/number%C2%A0of%C2%A0mba%C2%A0graduates%C2%A0in-the-us-per%C2%A0year/

OECD (2010) The high cost of low educational performance: the long-run economic impact of improving PISA outcomes, PISA/OECD Publishing [Online, accessed June 2012] www.sourceoecd.org/education/9789264077485

OECD (2011) Improving performance: leading from the bottom, PISA in focus 2011/2, OECD [Online, accessed June 2012] www.pisa.oecd.org/dataoecd/32/53/47271471.pdf. For more data and research, go to PISA 2009 results, learning trends: changes in student performance since 2000 (Volume V) [Online, accessed June 2012] www.oecd.org/document/60/0,3746,en_32252351_46584327_46609852_1_1_1_1,00.html

Orange (2009) Connected Britain – The face of working Britain in the digital age [Online, accessed June 2012] http://regmedia.co.uk/2009/09/02/orange_connected_britian.pdf

Pink, D H (2009) *Drive – The surprising truth about what motivates us*, Riverhead Books, A division of Penguin, New York

PwC (2010) 14th annual global CEO survey – growth reimagined, p 101 [Online, accessed June 2012] www.pwc.com/gx/en/corporate-strategy-services/publications/ceosurvey-innovation.jhtml

Schein, E H (2009) *Corporate Culture Survival Guide*, p 21, John Wiley and Sons, London

Scrimenti, M (2010) China business schools hit their stride, *Bloomsberg Businessweek*, 16 December [Online, accessed June 2012] www.businessweek.com/stories/2010-12-16/china-business-schools-hit-their-stridebusinessweek-business-news-stock-market-and-financial-advice

Singapore Business Review (2011) 92% of Singapore companies fail to meet corporate governance standards, 11 July [Online, accessed June 2012] http://sbr.com.sg/professional-services/news/92-singapore-companies-have-poor-corporate-governance

Soares, R *et al* (2010) 2010 Catalyst Census: Fortune 500, Women Executive Officers and Top Earners [Online, accessed June 2101] www.catalyst.org/publication/459/2010-catalyst-census-fortune-500-women-executive-officers-and-top-earners

Stewart Black, J (2009) Waging and winning the war for talent in Asia in *Leadership in Asia*, edited by Dave Ulrich, p 111

Tonello, N and Rabimov, S (2010) Conference Board, 2010 institutional investment report: trends in asset allocation and portfolio composition, p 22, The Conference Board [Online, accessed June 2012] www.conference-board.org/publications/publicationdetail.cfm?publicationid=1872

Towers Watson (2010) *The New Employment Deal, Insights from the 2010 Global Workforce Study*

United Nations, Department of Economic and Social Affairs, Population Division (2011) *World Population Prospects: The 2010 Revision* [CD-ROM] The United Nations

World Bank Group (2011) The worldwide governance indicators (WGI) project [Online, accessed June 2012] http://info.worldbank.org/governance/wgi/index.asp

World Bank Group (2012) School enrollment, tertiary (% gross) [Online, accessed June 2012] http://data.worldbank.org/indicator/SE.TER.ENRR

WorldatWork and Towers Watson (2010) Creating a sustainable rewards and talent management model – results of 2010 global talent management and rewards study [Online, accessed June 2012] www.worldatwork.org/waw/adimLink?id=42295

Yale University (2010) 2010 EPI (environmental performance index) report, p 6, Yale Center for Environmental Law & Policy, Yale University & Center for International Earth Science Information Network (CIESIN), Columbia University [Online, accessed June 2012] http://epi.yale.edu

FURTHER READING

Chesbrough, H W (2003) Open Innovation: The new imperative for creating and profiting from technology, 1 March, *Harvard Business Press*

Hammer, M and Champy, J (1993) *Reengineering the Corporation: A manifesto for business revolution*, Harper Business, New York

Senge, P M (1990) *The Fifth Discipline Fieldbook: Strategies and tools for building a learning organization*, Doubleday, New York

Strauss, W and Howe, N (1991) *Generations*, William Morrow and Company, New York

INDEX

Numbers in *italics* indicate a table or figure in the text